Sources for the History of Houses

John H Harvey

British Records Association

Archives and the User   No 3

1974

ARCHIVES AND THE USER

1 THE RECORDS OF THE ESTABLISHED CHURCH IN ENGLAND
by Dorothy M. Owen. 1970. 80p.

2 INDEXING FOR EDITORS by R. F. Hunnisett. 1972. £1.50.

3 SOURCES FOR THE HISTORY OF HOUSES
by John H. Harvey. 1974. £1.20.

Further titles in preparation

ISBN 0900222 04 2

Orders and enquiries should be addressed to the British Records Association, Master's Court, The Charterhouse, Charterhouse Square, London, EC1M 6AU.

Printed in England by
E.G.M.Mann & Son Ltd., Fordham Printers, Fordham, Ely, Cambs.

TABLE OF CONTENTS

FOREWORD

To the man in the street Research is dryasdust, but Detection breathes romance. Yet the two words, if not precisely synonyms, stand for two aspects of the same human activity. Detection is not exclusively concerned with crime, and research is carried on by others than atomic scientists and academics. It is a game at which, to a lesser or greater extent, anyone can play. Two fields for research - or detection - lie close at hand: genealogy, the tracing of ancestors; and the history of houses, the homes in which those ancestors lived. For the first there is a vast literature and the amateur genealogist does not lack for guidance. Strangely enough, however, little has been written on the subject of building history as a pursuit, and still less that helps the beginner.

This booklet is an attempt to fill the gap, based on practical experience over many years and in different parts of the country. Much of the background work was done as a beginner, and the results are addressed mainly to amateurs who need some help at starting. Very many institutions and persons have contributed directly or indirectly and acknowledgments are made and thanks returned especially to:

His Grace the Archbishop of Canterbury and the Church Commissioners for permission to use material in the Lambeth Palace Library; to the Warden and Fellows of Winchester College; to the National Trust in respect of manorial and estate records; the Principal Probate Registry and the Public Record Office; the Surrey Record Office; the Winchester Diocesan Registry in respect of records now in the Hampshire Record Office; the Borthwick Institute, York; the York City Library, particularly for access to the York City Archives; and York Minster Library.

Among the multitude of individuals to whom I am personally grateful I must name the late T. D. Atkinson, the late Herbert Chitty and the late L. F. Salzman; and Mr C. B. L. Barr, the Ven. C. R. Forder and Mr Maurice Smith; as also Mr and Mrs A. E. B. Owen for much helpful advice and for Mr Owen's care and hard work on editing and production.

J. H. H.

September, 1973

INTRODUCTION

In the last generation there has been a great increase of public interest in the past and in the means of finding out about it.* Archaeology, local history, biography and genealogy have experienced a boom which still continues. These are subjects in which the amateur may make as important discoveries as the professional, provided always that he first acquires some basic knowledge of how to set about his task. He seeks to know, but as an amateur searcher he must not only solve a particular problem, but discover how to set about the solution. The purpose of the present essay is to provide an elementary do-it-yourself kit for those who wish to answer the question: How can I find out the history of my house? A second purpose too may be served if it diverts from librarians and archivists even a small part of the increasing demand for help. The custodians of books and documents simply cannot be expected to spend enough time on each inquirer to answer all his questions. This is not their duty, though within reasonable limits they will gladly give some guidance. What they cannot do is to teach the elements of the subject. Archivists in particular, in the struggle against time to list and to index the incoming flow of records, are sometimes driven to insist that searchers must either do their own work, or else employ a professional for the purpose.

The amateur, once he has mastered the elements, will be able to deal with nine-tenths of the records he meets without more outside help than he is likely to get in the friendly society of search-rooms. Two bugbears must first be dealt with: palaeography, and Latin. The ability to read old forms of handwriting can be acquired piecemeal as research pushes the inquiry further and further back. As far as concerns documents of the last three hundred years, there is no problem beyond that of careless handwriting, a difficulty even more serious today than it was in the long period of italic and 'copperplate' hands. When, working backwards, the age of secretary hand is reached, elementary manuals are forthcoming.[1] As regards knowledge of Latin, it is not usually necessary until the search has gone beyond 1733: all legal documents previously in Latin have since then been kept in English. When Latin is met with, the subject must be tackled on its merits and according to the searcher's degree of knowledge, or total ignorance. Here again an introductory manual is available,[2] and goes far to solve the commonplaces found repeatedly.

The history of houses is based upon records of many different kinds and may be confirmed and amplified by non-documentary evidence. We are here concerned with the practical use of the sources and not with their nature. This is not a study of classes of archives but of the information which they yield tending towards a single end-product. Something must be said of the intended scope of this pamphlet and of its limitations: it is not a treatise of architectural history but designed to help the ordinary occupier of a house of some age - built before about 1850. Some quite modern buildings have historical interest,

---

*No general bibliography has been attempted, as it would largely duplicate the material in the following notes. In most relevant fields the best guide for the amateur is the *English Local History Handlist* (Historical Association, Helps for Students of History, no. 69, 4th edition, 1969). For those who wish to acquire a knowledge of the wider historical background, a good introduction is R. B. Pugh, *How to write a Parish History* (1954).

[1] Notably *How to read Local Archives 1550-1700*, by F. G. Emmison (Historical Association, 1967).

[2] E. A. Gooder, *Latin for Local History* (1961). See also R. E. Latham, 'The Banishment of Latin from the Public Records', *Archives,* iv no. 23 (1960), 158-69.

but it will either be notorious, or can easily be discovered from printed sources. The nearest public library should be consulted. Houses of outstanding architectural interest, of all dates, have generally been the subject of published studies.[3]

It may be as well to start with the main questions it is hoped to answer:

(1)   When was the house built; and when subsequently altered or enlarged?

(2)   Who built, enlarged or altered it?

(3)   What families have owned it?

(4)   Who have been the actual occupiers?

(5)   With what events of interest can it be associated?

Some questions may defy all attempts at an answer and in any case the final result may amount to very little. The student must be prepared for this and undertake the search for its own sake.

Setting aside large mansions and manor-houses, most other dwellings can be grouped, simply for purposes of research, into five main classes:

(A)   Rectories, vicarages and church houses;

(B)   Freehold houses, including those occupied on lease by tenants;

(C)   Copyholds; that is to say properties held under the former manorial system 'by copy of court roll';

(D)   Tenements subordinate to some larger house and occupied on short-term tenancies or at will: e.g. 'tied' farm cottages;

(E)   Houses formed by the conversion of non-domestic buildings such as barns, chapels, factories, mills or stables.

Another important practical distinction, cutting across these classes, is into urban and rural properties. Some types of record exist only for towns or only for country districts while others are more likely to be rewarding in one case or the other.

The most important basic rule is to work from the known to the unknown. Unproven statements or traditions, however romantic or attractive, should never be accepted without careful check of the sources, as they can lead to great waste of time in following false trails. At the start only one thing is positively known: the house itself with its name, number or description. The house must first be clearly *identified* in records of earlier periods, and this is often quite difficult. The traps laid for the unwary by official changes of street numbering are fairly obvious; but a more insidious snare has been set by owners who have renamed a house to which they have moved with the name of their previous dwelling in the same parish. Thus verbal descriptions cannot be accepted at face value but have to be tested to make sure that they do correspond with the building studied.

---

[3] See the relevant volumes of the Victoria County Histories; of the Inventories of the Royal Commissions on Ancient and Historical Monuments (separate series for England, Wales, Scotland); and the latest annual cumulative index to *Country Life*, for articles on individual mansions and country homes. The county volumes of N. Pevsner, *Buildings of England* (1951-) give much detail for works of the nineteenth and twentieth centuries. For regional and local surveys of old buildings see also J. H. Harvey, *Conservation of Old Buildings: a select bibliography* (Ancient Monuments Society, reprint from Transactions, xvi, 1969/1972), items 167-99, 210-11.

PART I

DOCUMENTARY EVIDENCE

The first step is to read the current title deeds which pass with the house, and which must be accepted as relating to it. Even these demand some caution if a parcel of 'old title' is included. Some early deeds may have been wrongly identified with the property. This is often due to the accumulation in a single ownership of many separate properties leased or rented out to tenants; conveyances describing the whole group then intervene between the early individual title deeds and those of separate properties sold off at different dates. It is, therefore, only the modern deeds and the accompanying Abstract of Title, upon which the student can implicitly rely. From them it should be possible to obtain a short description of the house, its position, and dimensions of the plot or curtilage on which it stands, with names of one or more previous owners and occupiers and very likely of the owners and occupiers of the adjacent properties by which it is bounded. It has up to now been assumed that the current title deeds are accessible, but this may not be so. If the inquirer is a tenant he will have to apply to his landlord for permission to inspect the deeds, making it clear that his interest is purely historical. Since there is generally no legal right of inspection it is open to the landlord to decline. In that case ownership of the property during the last hundred years or so must for the time being be left open. Most of the occupiers can often be traced from printed directories and the gaps filled in from official electoral rolls (see below, p. 30 and note 55).

Before going further the house should be traced back on successive editions of the large-scale Ordnance Survey plans, and a sketch made to show its relation to the local topography: natural features, roads, tracks and other buildings. Fortunate cases are where the site lies at a cross-roads or junction of any kind, next to a churchyard or to an inn or public house, or beside a quarry or marlpit. In such instances difficulties of identification are much reduced. Only the latest large-scale O. S. plans mark street-numbering, and where changes in numbering have been made it is necessary to study the numbers in a whole street or block through all available directories and electoral lists, to establish with certainty the correct number of a house at a given date. Care must be taken over errors in compilation of directories, and even of official registers of voters, and also against the misleading appearance of continuous tenure which occasionally conceals removal from one house into the house next door.

As the whole country has been covered by the O. S. plans on large scales since roughly the middle of last century, this stage of the search is the same in all cases.[4] It is almost always possible to establish the block-plan of the house as it was a century ago, and often to give it a name if it was in the countryside or a number if it lay in a town. Depending on the date to which the chain of title stretches, it may also be possible to name owner and occupier at roughly the same date and to check the name of the occupier (though seldom that of the owner) from directories and other printed sources. To consolidate this

[4] For the Ordnance Survey maps and plans see J. B. Harley in *Amateur Historian*, v no. 5, 130-40 (1-inch scale); no. 7, 202-11 (6-inch and 25-inch scales).

information and to obtain or confirm the name of the owner, the next stage is to find a plan which not only marks the building, but states the names of both owner and occupier at a given date.

Tithe Maps

For a great part of the country such plans exist in the series of Tithe Awards and Apportionments, made parish by parish, mostly within a few years around 1840. Though made under an Act of 1836 to establish the amounts of tithe payable on every parcel of land, these awards and their accompanying maps - surveyed on very large scales - are of vital importance for other purposes. More often than not they provide the essential starting point for historical research on individual buildings. Although few of the Tithe Maps were printed, they were made in triplicate along with the accompanying award and apportionment, and one or other of the copies is always accessible. The three copies were destined: (1) a national copy, for the Tithe Commissioners; now accessible, by giving notice in advance, at the Public Record Office; (2) a diocesan copy, now usually in the diocesan record office; (3) a copy for the parish, kept at the church, but later sometimes transferred to the custody of the civil parish authorities or to the diocesan or county record office.

In spite of their widespread availability the tithe records suffer from one inherent disadvantage: they were not concerned with any land freed from tithe before the award made under the 1836 Act.[5] Some land, usually that of a former monastic house, had been tithe-free from the Middle Ages, but a good deal of tithe was commuted much later in the course of legal enclosure of lands previously open or held in common. In such cases details can be found from the Enclosure Map and Award, so long as they exist and can be located.[6] But what if the property was in a tithe-free area and no previous enclosure can be discovered? Other maps provided with schedules of owners and occupiers were made for various reasons. A few surviving examples are concerned with parliamentary voting rights attached to 'burgage' tenements in ancient boroughs. Many more were made when Improvement Commissioners were appointed in a borough or town, as they were almost essential in connection with paving, sewerage and the laying of water and gas supplies and assigning responsibility for upkeep on the frontagers. Sometimes there was a general survey made privately for the lord of a manor or proprietor of a large estate, consisting of a large map with a reference book of all owners and occupiers. Many such maps are in the British Museum and in local libraries and record offices, but others are in private hands and hard to find. Some may be difficult of access even when found. Another possible source may be available when the property lies near any public undertaking, such as a canal or a railway. The required information may well be found on the deposited plans of the undertaking, which have detailed schedules of all the affected owners and

[5] For a full account of tithe records see W. E. Tate, *The Parish Chest* (3rd ed., 1969), chapter iv; also L. M. Munby in *History,* liv no. 180, 68-71; and J. B. Harley in *Amateur Historian,* vii no. 8, 265-74 (covering both enclosure and tithe maps).

[6] For enclosure awards and maps see W. E. Tate in *History,* li no. 172, 179-82, and his handlists for many counties. In other cases there are separately produced lists, and the county and local record offices should be consulted for most of the surviving maps. In the exceptional case of the West Riding of Yorkshire (which has no county record office) a detailed handbook, *West Riding Enclosure Awards* (1965) has been prepared jointly by the two County Committees of the National Register of Archives.

occupiers.[7] This is because it was customary for such surveys to include adjacent properties to allow for some variation in the final line chosen; purchase did not necessarily take place. Hence marginal information, relevant to the history of properties on either side of the line, has been preserved.

Rate Books

Up to now we have been dealing with sources of information which generally survive, and are accessible, for most properties. Regrettably this is by no means the case with the parochial assessments to rates which, if completely preserved, would provide a continuous list of occupiers and, from the introduction of an improved form for the new Poor Rate after 1834, of owners too. In fact it is extremely rare to find a full series of rate books for any one parish, even for the modern period after c. 1840-50. Nevertheless, it is common to find a sufficient number of books made up from different series: church rate, poor rate, highway rate, etc., to provide more or less continuous evidence back to a date in the second half of the eighteenth century. Although research may be pursued along other channels, it is impossible to over-estimate the importance of the rating assessments, and worth spending ample time on the search for rate books. When they are altogether missing before some modern date it may mean that all were deliberately destroyed, but often it indicates simply that their place of storage, such as a parish chest, has been forgotten or overlooked. Parish documents were formerly quite commonly kept at the home of a churchwarden or clerk.

In the Greater London Boroughs and in the larger cities and towns the surviving rate books have often been deposited in public libraries. This generally applies to books of the poor rate, long ago transferred from the custody of the church vestry to the civil parish authorities. Other rate books which had been kept in the church, or in the parsonage, may also have been deposited at the library. Unfortunately for the searcher it is more common to find that the civil and ecclesiastical records, if deposited, are in two different places: church rate books, vestry minutes and churchwardens' accounts and the like are now often to be found in the diocesan record office - frequently but not always associated with the county record office. In rural areas it is wise to consult the diocesan and/or county record office in the first instance. It is in the countryside that the greatest difficulties are likely to be encountered. In many parishes the surviving records are kept in the church and access is possible only by special arrangement with the incumbent. The rector or vicar, his curate or a churchwarden, will usually have to be present to invigilate the student while he is using the books. This may not be easy to arrange and may give rise to a claim for reasonable fees or a subscription to church funds. Although there is a statutory right (going back to 1744) to inspect rate books,

[7] For the older large-scale engraved maps see E. M. Rodger, *The Large Scale County Maps of the British Isles 1596-1850* (Oxford, Bodleian Library, 1960); for estate maps see F. G. Emmison in *History*, xlviii no. 162, 34-7; A. R. H. Baker in *Amateur Historian*, v no. 3, 66-71; J. B. Harley, *ibid.*, vii no. 7, 223-31. The most likely place to find deposited plans of public undertakings is the House of Lords Record Office, but those delivered to clerks of the peace are now generally in county record offices.

a cautious and tactful approach is to be recommended. In cases of serious difficulty the tentative suggestion may be made that the books be deposited for a limited period in the diocesan record office. It has to be faced that, on the rare occasions when even this suggestion fails, there may be no effective remedy.

To some extent the method of work on the books, when found, may have to be adapted to the circumstances. If the records are all in a library or record office to which an adequate number of visits can easily be paid, it is best to work methodically backwards, year by year, from a basic date in relatively modern times. From what has already been said, this date may well be in the period around 1840-1850, coinciding with the detailed information obtained from the tithe map and award or from other sources of the mid-nineteenth century. Assuming that the case is of the most difficult type, where the property sought is in the middle of a long unbroken street or block, it is essential to start by listing in order from one end of the block to the other the whole of the properties with the names of occupiers and the assessment (gross or rateable, consistently) for each. A copy of the relevant section of the tithe map or other detailed plan, or failing such, of the largest available Ordnance Survey plan (10.56 feet, 5 feet, or 25 inches to the mile) should be marked to correspond to the list. In cases where there is no available tithe map, or other plan giving the names of occupiers of individual parcels, it will probably be necessary to make use at the same time of information from street directories and perhaps from the electoral rolls (see Appendix A).

In the larger towns and cities the regular succession of houses along the main streets is often broken by the interpolation of groups of small premises built over the former yards or gardens of the larger 'front' houses. Great care has to be taken in such cases, especially if the house whose history is sought is itself in a yard, passage-way or lane off the street. Whereas the houses along the main frontage were usually listed in straightforward order from one end of the street to the other (though not always in the same direction in all rates), the houses in yards were sometimes set down from the front, sometimes starting at the back, and occasionally in no particular sequence. A rough-and-ready check on the probability of identification can often be made by comparing the amounts of the assessments with the size of the houses and plots on the map. Although far from accurate, this will commonly show that certain houses were of far higher value than the average and these should correspond either to notable mansions, or to houses with larger gardens than the standard town curtilages of more or less uniform width.

Even when a good series of rate books has survived, there may be problems. The most serious of these is where the parish is interrupted by parts of another parish. Normally this cannot be deduced from study of the rate books themselves, but only from a map which marks all boundaries of ancient parishes significant for rating purposes. Generally speaking both tithe maps and the first large-scale Ordnance Survey plans indicate ancient parish boundaries in full detail and, separately, the internal boundaries of rating areas (usually those of former parishes) into which a single parish may be divided. Although such cases complicate the problem by the need to discover two or more series of rate books, the position of the boundary - once fixed - is itself an important point of departure helping to establish the identity of the adjacent properties. Two other difficulties commonly arise. The more serious of these is often found in assessments of early date, where there is no regular topographical order, but an approximate ranking by the amount of assessment, the largest houses in the parish being placed first. Although valuable information can sometimes be obtained from rates set out in this way, they are rarely of much use in evidencing the history of a single property. On a smaller scale is the nuisance caused by the grouping together of several properties rated to the same person. This commonly occurred when the occupier of a house also paid rates on one or more parcels of land elsewhere in the parish. So long as only one house is included in the entry, this will not stand in the way of clear identification. But when, as sometimes happened, two or more houses were rated to the owner-occupier of one of them who was landlord to the short-term tenants of the rest, serious confusion may occur. This applies more particularly to the *absence* of these secondary houses from their places in the streets to which they belong.

From what has been said it will be evident that any given rate book has to be studied on its merits, and the methods used by its compilers deduced from a preliminary study. Where the book belongs to the (exceptional) class of truly methodical surveys, each section of it will begin with the name of a ward or other sub-section of the parish, or of a street, even naming the end or corner at which the list begins. In the case of large urban parishes a great deal of time can be saved by noting carefully the relationship of the particular house sought to the beginning of one of the main sections of assessment. Even before the end of the eighteenth century the collection of the rates in such areas had become a highly specialized occupation and so had given rise to better arrangement of the books. In the smaller rural parishes a more or less arbitrary 'round' of the houses, without subdivisions, might survive until the middle of the nineteenth century. Such simple rural rates are often the most difficult to use for historical purposes: they reduced the facts recorded to an absolute minimum; were often changed according to the convenience or the whim of the amateur officers who collected; and were often carelessly written.

The importance of working backwards from a given date, such as 1850, has to be stressed, for two main reasons. The first is that, as already stated, research must proceed from the known and clearly established towards the unknown. But secondly there is another very practical reason why the tabulation of entries from rate books should begin at the end: the almost universal tendency of vacant sites between houses to be filled with new buildings as time goes on. By working backwards - preferably from right to left in columns across the page - the gaps existing before given houses were built declare themselves automatically, and can often be confirmed from the evidence of maps, directories and other dated sources. Beginning with the earliest available rate would mean that it was constantly necessary to interpolate fresh entries between those already listed, with resulting confusion and, from sheet to sheet, lack of alignment in the continuing entries which it is sought to equate over the whole period.

So long as the same system is consistently used throughout, no ambiguity need arise in marking identical entries with " " or a tick, but it is vital to make sure that the amount of the assessment, as well as the name, is unchanged. Change in the amount of assessment may be general throughout the parish, in which case it has no special significance for the history of each individual house. In cases where the overall picture of the rateable values remains the same, a changed value for a single house practically always implies structural alterations or additions, or even total rebuilding. The subdivision of one large property into two smaller tenements is also a frequent phenomenon; where the two new assessments exactly equal the previous valuation of the whole, the division was probably done by mere partitioning; but where the total has increased it may imply demolition and the building of two new houses on the old site. A great deal of the evidential value of rates lies in such information, which can very often be confirmed by study of the surviving fabric of the house. More will be said later of the correlation of structural and documentary evidence. Here it is only needful to mention that, besides evidence of subdivision - and occasionally of the joining of two adjacent houses to form one - increases in rateable value during the eighteenth century commonly indicated the refronting in brick of an older house; while early in the nineteenth century a frequent occurrence was the addition of an extra storey.

When access to the surviving rate books is difficult and it is essential to save time, it is permissible to note the whole list of names only at intervals of five years. Even so, it is advisable not to make rash assumptions in regard to the individual property under study, and the intervening rates should be checked for any alterations or discrepancies, so that for this property the details of occupiers and of assessments may be complete. It is useful to have complete lists also for the houses abutting on the property on each side, as this makes it possible to check incidental mentions of occupiers found in the title deeds, and thus to confirm their relevance to the property. The importance of such additional checks cannot be too strongly emphasized, for experience shows that the history of many houses is far from straightforward, and that a minor discrepancy may be the essential clue leading to the unravelling of a complication.[8] Notwithstanding difficulties of access, the searcher ought always to do his best to note at least general particulars of any body of old records to which he obtains access as an individual (i.e. documents not deposited in a record office or library).[9] The methods of keeping parish records tended to be confused, and it is necessary to glance through *all* old parish books, even though they may be labelled as e.g. vestry minutes, in case an assessment may have been entered in the wrong book. Occasionally there may be rewarding discoveries, such as a full valuation of the houses in the parish, or even a local census. Opportunities to take notes from such finds should be exploited to the full.

---

[8] For rate books see I. Darlington in *History*, xlvii no. 159, 42-5; this points out, among other useful information, that the first street numbering in the City of London and Liberties was in 1767. In most provincial towns the date was far later, c. 1825-50. At York, where the names of streets began to be put up at the corners 'as is done in London' in 1782 (William White, 'Analecta Eboracensia' MS., Yorkshire Philosophical Society Acc. no. 5031, p. 7), there was numbering only in New Bridge Street and Coney Street in 1823 (Baines's Directory). In the directory of 1818 no numbers are shown; they had been generally adopted by 1828 (Pigot's Directory).

[9] Provided that he can obtain the owner's consent, the searcher should deposit a copy of his notes with the National Register of Archives.

Tax Records

Along with rate books may be considered the records of some forms of taxation, notably the Land Tax,[10] Hearth Tax, and Window Tax.[11] As a general rule the land tax returns survive from 1780 and are a valuable source for the next fifty years. Unlike most early parish rate books, they give the names both of owners and of occupiers, but they are much less reliable as a source of connected history of houses. On the other hand, they often yield a great deal of additional information if studied after a continuous or more or less continuous list of occupiers has already been compiled. In a few counties there are land tax records from dates long before 1780, and at times there may be local copies preserved among the church or parochial documents. Similarly there may be local returns to the window tax kept with borough archives, along with copies of the hearth tax. The latter, as a major source, however, have to be studied in the Public Record Office except for areas where they are already in print. Neither the hearth tax nor the window tax returns can be used as a substitute for rate books, but they do provide much additional information of value for filling in detail, and also for study in relation to the building itself. Conclusions in regard to the dates of insertion of chimney stacks may be reached from the enumeration of hearths, while the number of windows taxed may confirm or disprove the tentative structural history drawn up for a given building.

Recapitulation

The types of record already described, so far as they survive in any given area, yield evidence for houses of all kinds, and it may be as well to take stock of the state of such general research before proceeding to consideration of the records that apply to each of the classes of building described (above, p. 6). The main stages of general search will by now have included:

(1) The identification of the house on the current Ordnance Survey plans of the largest scales, with its present street numbering or name, if any; and comparison with the plan of the site in all the earlier maps, printed or in manuscript, that can be discovered;

(2) The identification of the owner and occupier in the mid-nineteenth century from the tithe map or, in its absence, from other equivalent records;

(3) The filling in, as far as may be possible, of the complete list of owners and occupiers from c. 1850 to the present day, from the title deeds, abstract of title (often stretching back to a date earlier than that of the first original deed to be preserved), local directories and electoral rolls;

(4) The checking of this list with all accessible rate books and, where rating records survive from before c. 1850, the continuation of the series of occupiers back to the period of the earliest assessment in continuous series. This check should also cover the land tax records, generally accessible for the period 1780-1832 and occasionally further back.

[10] For records of the land tax see H. G. Hunt in *History*, lii no. 176, 283-6; D. Grigg in *Amateur Historian*, vi no. 5, 152-6; D. Iredale, *ibid.*, vii no. 6, 182-9. The earliest dates of assessment to land tax surviving among the official records for each county are given in *County Records* (Historical Association, H.62, 1967).

[11] The hearth tax returns are discussed by R. Howell in *History*, xlix no. 165, 42-5. Many returns for counties or cities have been printed, usually with explanatory introductions, by record societies.

In view of the very large proportion of houses built in the Georgian period or later, this programme may well have covered the whole history of the existing structure, but will have provided only a skeleton or scaffolding to be clothed by further research (see below, p. 30). Apart from such continued search for details of human or architectural interest, there remains the task of carring back the story, whether of the building or of the site on which it was built, to the beginning of documentary record. At this stage it is convenient to consider houses by categories, according to which of the five main classes (above, p. 6) they belong.

(A) *Former rectories and other church houses*

At the outset it is as well to be clear that the terms 'rectory' and 'vicarage' are used in two senses: not only of the house in which the incumbent lives, but of the system of administration of the parish (the 'cure of souls') involved in each case. Each early church was usually provided with an area of land (the glebe) from which the priest (in this case the rector) could support himself, along with the tithes (one-tenth of all produce) from the other lands in the parish. The rector, during his term of office, was legally possessed of the freehold of the 'living', that is of the church and the glebe land, inclusive of the rectory house built on a part of the glebe. In some large parishes the amount of glebe land was so great that the rector, even at an early date, made no attempt to cultivate it, but had it farmed by tenants. This gave rise to the phenomenon of the 'rectorial manor', where the rector was actually lord of a small manor within, but independent of, the principal manor (often but not always the same area as the ancient parish). The rector, besides being the parish priest responsible for the spiritual welfare of his parishioners, was in such cases also a landowner of some importance; and, until the beginning of the thirteenth century (when Rome began strictly to enforce the rule of clerical celibacy), the rectory might even be inherited from father to son.

When it was no longer possible to pass on a rectory to the priest's own son, there was a considerably greater inducement to win spiritual merit by devoting the profits of the rectory, considered as a lay estate, to religious purposes. This could be achieved by the gift of the rectory to a religious house (an abbey or priory) which, by obtaining licences from the King and from the Pope, was allowed to 'appropriate' the living for its own benefit. When this happened the monastery in its corporate capacity became rector, and had to provide a priest to look after the 'cure of souls' in the parish: this priest was a vicar, or substitute for the rector. A new system of legal entitlement grew up by which vicars were normally paid by receiving the 'small tithes' which notably included the tenth of the produce of all gardens and lands dug by the spade. In some cases a definite share or stipend was laid down for a particular vicar by the diocesan bishop, who 'ordained' a vicarage. Such an ordination (recorded in the bishop's register) might include a share of the glebe and the entitlement of the vicar to a house - sometimes the former rectory of the parish before appropriation, but at other times a separate house in another place.

At the Dissolution of the monasteries under Henry VIII, in 1536-40, all the rights of each foundation passed to the Crown. These rights included both the patronage (i.e. the right of presentation) of livings, and the freehold lands and tithes of appropriated rectories. When grants were made by the Crown to new lay landlords of the ex-monastic estates, these normally included such rectorial rights. The result was the creation, in the latter part of the sixteenth century, of a new category of 'lay rectors'. In any given case it is important to establish whether the status of the priest's house is that of a rectory (never appropriated), a lay rectory (appropriated to a monastery but later transferred to lay hands), or a vicarage. In this last case, and in the case of ancient rectories, there will certainly be some records in ecclesiastical repositories.[12] Mostly these will now be found in the relevant diocesan record offices, but a few may remain with the Church Commissioners, while others are to be found in parish chests or in the custody of the rector or vicar for the time being. Among the diocesan records two classes are of particular importance, so far as they survive: Glebe Terriers,[13] and Sequestration Papers. The terriers, of which copies sometimes exist in the parish registers or other church books, should include a description of the parsonage house, and this is commonly in sufficient detail, as to materials, number of rooms and other particulars, as to enable a good deal of the history of the building to be reconstructed. The records of sequestrations deal with the gap between one incumbency and the next, and may include detailed accounts for the repair of dilapidations and even, in exceptional cases of dispute, the accounts of expenditure on the house and garden by a parson during his incumbency. Similar records are sometimes preserved in connection with cases before ecclesiastical courts.

The church books,[14] sometimes at the church but very commonly kept at home by the incumbent and handed on to his successor, often include a compilation on the rectory or vicarage made at some earlier date. This, though not a primary record source, may save a great deal of time and trouble, and perhaps preserve texts or abstracts of original documents now lost. In cases where a rectory house has been rebuilt since the early eighteenth century there may be original plans and other documents connected with the rebuilding, either among the church records, or preserved in diocesan records. The classes of Faculty Books and Papers among diocesan records are always worth searching for stray entries of possible relevance. A special category of livings is formed by those which, during the Middle Ages, were appropriated to a 'secular' (i.e. collegiate) foundation. Such were the ancient secular cathedrals and the colleges of the two ancient Universities of Oxford (with Winchester College) and Cambridge (with Eton). In all such cases the most likely source of information (not necessarily the only source) is the archives of the cathedral chapter or college concerned. In this category there is a much greater likelihood than elsewhere of obtaining full information, from detailed accounts and correspondence, of alterations, rebuilding, or change of site of a rectory or vicarage.

Rectory houses which passed into lay ownership after the dissolution of the monasteries in the sixteenth century present an entirely different problem. The 'root of title' probably lies in the grant from the Crown of ex-monastic

[12] For ecclesiastical records generally see D. M. Owen, *The Records of the Established Church in England* (British Records Association, Archives and the User no. 1, 1970). The diocesan record office is the normal source of up-to-date information on the custody of ecclesiastical records. For records of the parish churches see W. E. Tate, *The Parish Chest* (above, note 5).

[13] For glebe terriers see D. M. Barratt in *History*, li no. 171, 35-8.

[14] Generally speaking, the records of the ancient parish other than the registers.

estates, and it is unusual for any earlier documents to survive. From the time of the grant onwards, the former rectory house - perhaps used as the mansion or chief messuage of a small manor - will have passed as an ordinary freehold property, either along with or separated from the rest of the monastic estate. As a dwelling of greater distinction, and perhaps larger size, than the average, an old rectory in this category may have found a place in county and local histories of various dates, but as far as record sources are concerned, it must be considered as belonging to the next class, that of freeholds.

(B) *Freehold houses, including those occupied on lease*
Tracing the descent of freehold properties of moderate size is generally a difficult matter. Although for centuries attempts were made to insist upon the registration of title in some form, this aim has only been achieved, legally, in the present century with the introduction of registered title in 1925,[15] and in practice many years must still elapse before its adoption is complete. For the historian it is important to note that there is no general right of inspection of the registers which, unless and until the law is amended, will not be available for purposes of research. This is, however, a problem essentially for the future, and hardly affects the student of the present day. The question is, therefore, how to discover surviving deeds, or other records of freehold transactions, in cases where the current title does not extend beyond the quite modern period (see Appendix B). Regrettably, this is the case with the vast majority of old houses, and it has to be admitted that the search is often a long and vain one. Search should, nevertheless, be made in the relevant county or local record offices and libraries, where large numbers of miscellaneous deeds are preserved, in addition to those which form integral parts of the deposited archives of estates great and small. To go beyond the limits laid down by the existing state of indexing in each repository it is often necessary to widen the search to cover surviving material for a whole parish or manor, and to read through unindexed reports on extensive groups of archives.[16]

Some county and other record publishing societies have printed texts or abstracts of deeds,[17] as well as many cartularies containing copies of deeds.[18] Although most cartularies relate to the Middle Ages and are only seldom relevant to the history of existing buildings, they provide vital information for a small minority of houses. Some private cartularies and estate registers cover more recent periods.[19] Another parallel source, also largely represented in printed abstracts, consists of the Feet of Fines.[20] The Fines, or Final

---

[15] The first general act enabling registration of title was passed in 1862 but proved ineffective; a further act of 1897 was very slowly adopted by county councils, starting with the administrative County of London by stages after 1898.

[16] For deeds see A. D. Carr in *History*, l no. 170, 323-8; H. Miles in *Amateur Historian*, iv no. 1, 26-7; and E. Legg, *ibid.*, vi no. 3, 86-90. Many deeds, particularly of the sixteenth and seventeenth centuries but also before and after, were registered by endorsement on the Close Rolls. These must be consulted at the Public Record Office.

[17] See E. L. C. Mullins, *Texts and Calendars* (Royal Historical Society, 1958), and R. Somerville, *Handlist of Record Publications* (British Records Association, Publications Pamphlet no. 3, 1951).

[18] For cartularies, both ecclesiastical and private, see G. R. C. Davis, *Medieval Cartularies of Great Britain* (1958).

[19] *Ibid.*, 140-56; and for example nos. 1190, 1203-4, 1278, 1316, 1321, 1332; also C. A. F. Meekings and P. Shearman, edd., *Fitznells Cartulary* (Surrey Record Society, vol. xxvi, 1968).

[20] For the Feet of Fines see R. E. Latham in *Amateur Historian*, i no. 1, 5-9; and refer to note 17 above (Somerville, sections 46, 86; Mullins, as indexed).

Concords, might have provided a satisfactory system of universal registration of title from the twelfth century onwards; that they were not used more widely in conveyancing is due to the rooted English objection to publicity regarding ownership of property. Furthermore, the fines that do exist give only a very loose description of the property conveyed, so that they fail to provide adequate proof of identity in those cases where no other evidence survives.

The search for old title must in most cases be guided by the particular circumstances. Specially helpful conditions prevail in certain areas and in London and most corporate towns. From early in the eighteenth century registries of deeds were set up for the county of Middlesex and for each of the three ridings of Yorkshire, at the respective county towns of Beverley, Northallerton, and Wakefield.[21] With relatively few exceptions, the volumes of 'memorials' in these registries contain abstracts of all conveyances of freehold property, both absolute (i.e. by way of sale or gift) and by way of mortgage. The relevant parts of all wills relating to the transfer of real estate are also registered. There are indexes to wills, to the vendors of properties, and to the parishes or townships in which properties lie. In the absence of indexes to purchasers in the earlier periods, it is often a complicated task to trace a particular property back, but the information does exist and, given time and patience, is forthcoming. The inclusion of wills is helpful in two ways: no search through the records of various courts of probate is needed, as the registration covers all relevant wills, regardless of where they may have been proved; and a few wills are found that were apparently never proved at all[22] (see Appendix C).

In London and most corporate towns there was, from time immemorial, a local customary right of bequeathing land by will, and in some cases this led to a system of civic registration, which extended also to deeds which the parties wished to enrol.[23] Such registration of deeds for greater security of title was fairly common during the Middle Ages, fell into at least relative desuetude, and was later revived.[24] Though very much less complete than the eighteenth-century system of registration introduced in Middlesex and Yorkshire, surviving civic registers contain copies or abstracts of many thousands of individual deeds and are a great help to the searcher. For the countryside in general nothing of the kind exists, but some gaps can be filled from other

[21] The Registries were set up in 1704 (West Riding), 1707 (East Riding), 1708 (Middlesex) and 1735 (North Riding). For the Deeds Registries see W. E. Tate in *Bulletin of the Institute of Historical Research*, xx (1943-45), 97-105. The records of the Middlesex Registry are held in part in the Greater London Record Office, in part in the Middlesex Records Office. The three Yorkshire Registries closed for legal purposes late in 1972, but arrangements have been made for continuing use by historical students.

[22] Wills that concerned *only* real estate (with personal property below the value of £5) did not have to be submitted to probate; but there is reason to think that, especially in the North of England, there was widespread evasion of payment of probate fees by executors who simply fulfilled the intent of the will to the satisfaction of the heirs and legatees.

[23] For London wills see R. R. Sharpe, ed., *A Calendar of Wills proved and enrolled in the Court of Husting, London, 1258-1688,* 2 vols. (1888-9). It is to be noted that this printed calendar omits much detail of importance, which can be studied in the MS. abstracts of wills and deeds, with elaborate indexes, available in the Corporation of London Records Office, Guildhall, London, E.C.2.

[24] As at York, where there are registers of or including deeds enrolled before the (Lord) Mayor from c. 1327 to 1633; and a revived series starting in 1719 and running on to 1866, but with few entries after 1832 (York City Archives, E.20: A/Y, B/Y, E.22, E.26-27, E.93-98). The mediaeval register of deeds for Winchester, covering the period 1303-1600, is in the British Museum (Stowe MS. 846).

sources. The Court Rolls of many manors, up and down the country, recorded transfers of freeholds in order that quitrents might be claimed from the right persons. In order to make use of such records it is necessary to establish the manor to which a given freehold was attached. This can be done with most ease and certainty from manorial surveys provided with maps, but in other cases reliance has to be placed on the cumulative evidence derived from court rolls, quit rentals, and records of other types.

Two other categories of secondary records may be particularly useful in supplying the place of missing deeds. Private acts obtained for the settlement of bankrupt and other estates often include a great deal of information drawn from the title deeds of the estate and its various parts.[25] At times the schedules to such acts amount to a detailed survey of every parcel of the property affected, and a good deal of the history of each part of the estate may be recorded. Information of a similar kind can often be found in records of the second category, the printed sale particulars issued by auctioneers and estate agents. A great many such particulars survive as individual copies kept with the title deeds to which they refer, but they may also be found in libraries, in private collections on local history, and in record offices; file copies still survive with many of the older firms of land and estate agents and surveyors. In a few cases printed particulars from as far back as the early years of the eighteenth century may be found, but the bulk of this material dates from after 1800.[26] Information of the same sort may also be found in newspaper advertisements (see below, p. 32).

It is not possible here to discuss the many different forms of conveyance,[27] but it may be useful to warn the student against certain traps. (1) Difficulty is commonly experienced when a deed names several persons as parties, either as vendors or as purchasers. Sometimes all of these persons acted as trustees on behalf of the real vendor or purchaser; but more often the group consists of the real party (and commonly his wife) and one or more persons acting as trustees. (2) Care must be taken to distinguish mortgages from outright grants: a chain of title may frequently include not only the absolute transactions, but also a parallel series of deeds conveying a mortgage on the property. (3) In the very common form of conveyance by 'Lease and Release' the 'Lease for one year' is a legal form and *not* a real lease; but it often names only the real parties and is therefore simpler to understand than the Release to which there might be many parties.

Leases and Tenancy Agreements
As has been seen, it is by no means easy to establish the descent of freehold title to a small property. The difficulties are even greater in regard to properties which, instead of being occupied by the owners, were leased to tenants. The

[25] See M. Bond on Estate Acts of Parliament in *History*, xlix no. 167, 325-8; and the *Index to Private Acts*. Many private acts of local interest are to be found in libraries and record offices, but some only in the House of Lords Record Office.
[26] Local record offices and libraries hold many sale particulars; for information on old firms the Royal Institution of Chartered Surveyors may be consulted.
[27] For conveyancing see A. Foster, *Conveyancing Practice from Local Records* (reprint from *Thoresby Miscellany*, xii part ii, Leeds, 1948); and for the main types of deeds A. A. Dibben, *Title Deeds 13th-19th Centuries* (Historical Association, H.72, 1968/1971); also A. D. Carr in *History*, l no. 170, 323-8.

reason for this is that, whereas there always was until quite modern times a legal incentive towards the preservation of deeds, short-term leases and tenancy agreements ceased to have any value beyond a comparatively short period. As far back as there are surviving rate books or records of the land tax and of certain other taxes, it is possible to learn the names of the *de facto* occupiers of houses or land as a more or less continuous series. Even further back there are likely to be mentions of specific occupiers at given dates in the deeds of the property or in those of abutting houses on either side. But no entries of these kinds yield information as to the *de jure* tenure of the occupiers, the dates when they entered and left, or the rents paid. It is true that the gross valuation in assessments was theoretically equal to the rental of the premises, and this is useful as a working approximation, but it is no more than that.

In the majority of cases there is no real hope of discovering the series of documents which conferred temporary rights upon occupiers, though indirect references to the terms of such records may be found in deeds, wills and memoranda. On the other hand, a substantial minority of leased premises belongs either to corporate bodies (mostly ecclesiastical and educational, but including also some of the greater London City Companies) or to great private estates. In such cases there is a very good chance of finding a whole series of texts of leases, in the form of registered copies, of loose counterparts, or of originals surrendered at expiration (see Appendix D). Continuous series of registers of leases, in book form, were normally kept in respect of church lands, on behalf of the bishops or chapters; and by the bursaries of university colleges and schools. In a few cases these series start as far back as the fourteenth century, though there seems to have been a wave of improved administration in such matters soon after the Dissolution of the monasteries, around 1550-60; but the earlier volumes have not always been preserved.[28] Private estates rarely kept registers, but preserved over long periods bundles of counterpart or surrendered leases, sometimes to be found deposited in record offices, still in muniment rooms, or in the offices of land agents, stewards or solicitors.

Most leases and analogous tenancy agreements belong to one or other of two main classes. On the one hand are individual leases without any right of renewal, and virtually all ordinary tenancy agreements: relatively ephemeral, these seldom form part of any regular system, and their survival is haphazard. Leases granted by corporations and by great estates, however, constituted in effect a form of continuous tenure, neither freehold nor copyhold, and commonly including a right of perpetual renewal.[29] The conditions of such leases varied greatly in different parts of the country and upon different estates. A very common form of renewable lease was granted for a moderate

[28] Some mediaeval registers including leases are mentioned by Davis (see note 18 above). The main series relating to cathedral estates are to be found among the chapter archives, but many passed to the Ecclesiastical Commissioners who have now distributed most of them to diocesan record offices. Besides the leases of property of the bishop and of the chapter there may also be separate series of leases or registers concerning property of other bodies such as Vicars Choral, as at York (Minster Library). For available lists of ecclesiastical records, see D. M. Owen in *Archives,* x no. 46 (1971), 53-6.

[29] For leases and tenancy agreements see P. Roebuck in *Local Historian,* x no. 1, 7-12; for leases for lives see H. Peskett in *Genealogists' Magazine,* xvii no. 6 (1973), 327-9.

term such as 21 years, with renewal after perhaps 7 years; leases of this sort are very usual in the case of town properties. Rural properties were in some districts commonly leased 'for lives', either with or without right of renewal at the end of the last life. This latter kind of leasehold seems to represent in many cases a transformation of earlier copyhold manors by deliberate policy. During the later Middle Ages the lords (often a monastic house) took into their demesne lands every copyhold that forfeited or fell in, and instead of re-granting it by copy in the manorial court, leased it out to a 'farmer' (so called because he paid a money rent or 'farm') on more profitable terms. In some cases several small copyholds might be joined together to form a larger farm, and some of the old houses would fall to ruin or be demolished for their materials. It is at any rate usual for early leaseholds to be substantial in area, though at a later date quite small properties might be let for lives.

Leases for lives seem at first to have been granted for the lives of several (generally three) members of a tenant family, and often with a right of substitution of a further life in return for a predetermined payment. Though satisfactory in periods of financial stability, and then equitable as between landlord and tenant, this unduly favoured the tenant in times of inflation. As far as possible, therefore, landlords tended later to limit the right of substitution or to allow for an increase in payments. Another development in some districts was the substitution, not of lives in the family of tenants, but of public figures, the date of whose death would be notorious. This added a trace of the fascination of a lottery or a tontine to the dry-as-dust formulae of the law. Those - and there were many of them - who inserted the life of H.R.H. the late Duke of Connaught (1850-1942), were lucky in his longevity. It should be obvious that considerable care must be taken in perusing the text of leases of this kind, to discover the real beneficiaries and to distinguish them from the named lives. A further complication arises from the increasing tendency to sub-let such leased properties.[30] The sub-letting was usually by short-term agreements, now lost, and there is no clear expectation that the leaseholder was, at any rate from the eighteenth century onwards, also the actual occupier.

(C) *Copyhold houses and customary tenures*
Fortunately for those interested in the smaller houses of early date (i.e. built before about 1800), a large proportion of them was held by copy of court roll under the manorial system. Since hardly any surviving houses were built before 1300, it is not necessary here to consider the origins of the system or its rather obscure links with servile social status in the Middle Ages. The system as it is found in the earliest court rolls, of the middle of the thirteenth century, remained fundamentally unchanged until its extinction after 1925. Apart from the change of language from Latin to English during the Commonwealth, and again after 1733, the basic essentials of the court roll and of the transactions it recorded stayed the same for seven centuries. Mastery of the forms used in English during the last two hundred years of the system, with only a very elementary study of Latin and of court hand, opens up to the student the whole range of manorial documents that may be available.

[30] The occupying families may sometimes be discovered in the Census Returns from 1841 onwards, but their association with particular premises is generally obscure.

Each manor had its own customs, which had the force of law, and though the general pattern remained constant, the differences between one manor and the next are a continuing source of interest. The discrepancies were concerned mainly with two things: the system of inheritance, and the rights of the tenants. Outside Kent, where a system of partition of holdings between all the children ('gavelkind') was in force, there were two main types of inheritance in English manors: to the youngest son ('Borough English'), and to the eldest son by way of primogeniture (in a few documents referred to as 'French Borough'). There is a presumption that Borough English was widespread if not universal in early times, but that after the Norman Conquest primogeniture spread, in imitation of freehold inheritance. On the average, the succession of the youngest son was to the advantage of the tenant family, since it tended to postpone the next payment of succession dues. It might, therefore, be thought that the change to primogeniture was calculated policy on the part of lords of manors, or their stewards; yet there is evidence that in fact the change was sometimes made in response to pressure from the tenants, who were prepared to pay a substantial lump sum for the privilege. It can only be supposed that this represents a sense of 'snob value' in having the same custom as freeholders.[31]

The rights of the tenants were largely in matters relating to the communal farming of the land, but affected houses in various ways. In many manors the copyholder might use timber growing on his holding for the repair of his house, but often with the reservation that oak timber might only be used by specific licence from the lord. Tenants of more than one holding might, by licence, take down a framed house or barn from one tenement and re-erect it upon another.[32] Neglect or unauthorized alteration of the house or subsidiary buildings, or felling of oak timber, were generally accounted 'waste' and punishable by forfeiture of the holding.[33] Normally tenants were given fair warning in the manorial court of neglect or other failure in their duties, a suspended fine being imposed if they did not put matters right before the next sitting of the court. The 'homage' of the manor, that is the body of copyholders who were bound as a condition of their tenure ('suit of court') to attend, were under an express duty to present all offences against the custom of the manor, without fear or favour.[34]

In essence the system of succession was extremely simple. When a copyholder died, his estate owed to the lord a heriot consisting of the best beast on the estate, or a fixed sum of money for which the heriot had been commuted. At the next court held after the death, the homage presented it,

[31] For example the tenants of Great Bookham, Surrey, in 1339 profferred 40s. to the Abbot of Chertsey's steward to obtain the right of succession by primogeniture; see E. Toms, ed., *Chertsey Abbey Court Rolls Abstract* (Surrey Record Society, vol. xxi, 1954, no. 1047 and Introduction, p. xiii); several other manors of the abbey obtained the same 'privilege' in succession.

[32] The importance of court rolls as evidence of building and rebuilding was pointed out by G. Eland, *At the Courts of Great Canfield, Essex* (1949), a pioneer study; and see Appendix F.

[33] The court rolls of Little Bookham, Surrey, include an instance of forfeiture in 1664 (court of 7 October) by William Thornborough, a mortgagee who on acquiring a copyhold by foreclosure (court of 18 October 1655) had proceeded to fell the timber for profit and so lost the holding altogether (Surrey Record Office).

[34] The full procedure of manorial courts, as held in this century by the Steward of the Manors of Winchester College, was recorded by the late Herbert Chitty, the last Steward, and is printed in J. H. Harvey, *The Mediaeval Architect* (1972), 257-61.

and proclamation was made for the heir to come forward to be admitted. If he did so, he paid the heriot and also a fine (usually in money and more or less arbitrary, though it had to be 'reasonable' in relation to the current value of money and the fine paid by the previous holder), for admission. He was then admitted 'by the rod', a billet of wood, staff, pen or other object being placed in his hands by the steward, and had to 'do fealty' to the lord, promising to pay the accustomed rent (usually a very small sum of money) and perform the services due from the tenement. Although in the Middle Ages there had been extensive services due, to be performed on the lord's land, these had by the fifteenth century been very widely commuted into money payments added to the rent. For a long time, until the middle of the seventeenth century, it is common to find that eggs and poultry might form part of the annual rent, but in the end these too were turned into a small cash payment. For purposes of tracing back the history of a tenement it is particularly important to note the amount of the rent which, unlike the fine, remained constant and thus assists in identification when manorial rentals have been preserved. Sometimes the individual holdings were known by names, but these tended to be those of former copyholding families, and in course of time were superseded.

Although in theory the early customary tenants had been 'bound to the soil' and so their houses would descend in the same family indefinitely, a great deal of buying and selling is found even in the earliest surviving court rolls. Formally, the copyholder had to 'surrender' his tenement to the lord, with an expression of intent, e.g. for the benefit of a purchaser or of a mortgagee, or to the uses of his own last will. In the case of outright sale by this method, a heriot or its cash equivalent was payable by the vendor, and the fine for admission by the purchaser. One of the most helpful features of the system is that copyhold tenure was personal, and the property could only be sub-let by express licence, which was entered, with the sum paid for the privilege, on the court roll. Most earlier licences name the particular person to whom the tenement might be sub-let, but later open licences were issued and there is no evidence of the actual occupier. Fortunately this practice is most found at a period when the names of occupiers can generally be discovered from other sources.

Court Rolls

In practice the problems of research in copyhold history are those of survival and accessibility of court rolls. Very nearly every part of the country, except corporate towns, came within the system, so that in theory there should be a series of court rolls for each manor, starting at a date between 1250 and 1300 perhaps, and coming down to 1925 or later. Only in a very few manors do records survive even approximately according to this pattern. Gaps of greater or less extent are common, and in many cases the surviving rolls start only in the sixteenth century or later. After about 1800 many copyholds were enfranchised, that is converted to freehold tenure, so that the record of transfers comes to an end. All the same, court rolls in reasonably complete series do survive for a great many manors between roughly the time of the Civil War, c. 1650, and the middle of the nineteenth century, when the final decline of the system set in. Thus the evidence does exist for the story of a large proportion of small houses in rural areas. Obtaining access to this evidence is another matter.

The first step is to discover the manor to which a particular house belonged, and this may not be easy. It is unusual for documents concerned with non-manorial matters to make any reference to the manorial allegiance of a property. In many parts of the country there was one chief manor more or less equivalent to the area of the ancient parish, and in such areas there is a strong probability that houses in the parish belonged to the manor too. The exceptions are mainly concerned with subordinate or reputed manors which had the right of holding their own courts, and in that case it may be necessary to search through several sets of records. The most conclusive evidence is that of a chain of current title which goes back to a deed of enfranchisement of a former copyhold or refers to such enfranchisement in an Abstract or in annexed Sale Particulars. In all other cases an attempt should be made to discover a manorial map of the area, surveyed for some former lord. As such maps commonly survive with the other manorial records: court rolls, rentals, and written surveys (see Appendix E), one search may result in the discovery of all the relevant documents at once. Many sets of court rolls have now been deposited in county record offices, and others from ecclesiastical lords, in diocesan record offices. Still others are in public libraries, the libraries of some cathedrals, the British Museum, Bodleian Library, and — mostly those of royal manors and those of the Duchy of Lancaster — in the Public Record Office. Normally the first enquiry should be made at the relevant county record office, but it is advisable in all cases of difficulty to apply to the Royal Commission on Historical Manuscripts.[35]

Once found, the court rolls present the problem of search (see Appendix F). During the Middle Ages the records actually were on parchment rolls, but at a date between about 1550 and 1650 most stewards took to keeping the records in books. While the rolls are seldom indexed, there is commonly an index in each book, or a separate index kept with the series of books. In other cases there is an internal system of reference, forward and back, entered in the record of transfers or in the margins. If there is no form of index it is necessary to go through the text, helped by such marginal titles as may have been entered, and by looking for known names among the Homage set out at the head of each court held. Copyholders not present may be found entered under the separate headings of Essoins (excused on sending a reasonable excuse, usually illness) or Amercements (fines for non-attendance without satisfactory excuse). Where a good series of Rentals survives, this may be a short cut to the names of tenants at given dates. A manorial survey, especially when provided with a map, affords an opportunity to check the results obtained by search through the rolls. Since it was usual for the stewards, or their clerks, to keep a rough record of the courts in minute books, and to have the full record engrossed later, it is not uncommon for both series of books to survive, or for the minute books to survive (perhaps kept by a firm of solicitors) when the official series has been lost. It is most advisable to check entries in both sets of books whenever possible, since scribal mistakes crept in during engrossment.

[35] The offices of the Royal Commission, with the associated National Register of Archives, are at Quality House, Quality Court, Chancery Lane, London, W.C.2. Reference may also be made to the standard, but largely outdated, book by N. J. Hone, *The Manor and Manorial Records* (2nd ed., 1912); and to H. A. Doubleday and W. Page, *A Guide to the Victoria History of the Counties of England* (1903), which includes lists of court rolls in the British Museum. See also W. F. Mumford, 'Studying Medieval Court Rolls', *Local Historian*, x no. 2, 83-7.

The methods of keeping courts and of recording the business are remarkably uniform over the whole country, and experience gained anywhere is serviceable for all manorial records. The only major difference found between different sets of court rolls is that between the ordinary series concerned with a single manor, and the 'omnibus' type of books kept for some corporate lords in respect of all their manors. In such cases the steward kept up a round of visits to each manor in turn, on a basis of geographical convenience, and had the records of all courts entered *seriatim* in a single set of books.[36] Although this system may be rather more cumbersome to consult, the indexes are commonly better, and subsidiary series of reference books, summarising the descents of individual holdings, may be available in addition.[37] Surveys often specify the materials of which houses are built, and the number of bays in barns, as well as enumerating all other outbuildings.

(D) *Subordinate tenements*
Manorial and other large estates, and substantial farms, usually had a number of small houses and cottages occupied by members of the estate staff or by agricultural labourers. On large estates there is a reasonable chance that detailed records of estate administration may survive, including even drawings and specifications for the building of such houses, and detailed accounts of the costs of erection. In other cases an estate or farm may have taken over freehold or copyhold properties originally independent, whose earlier history at any rate may be found in a set of title deeds or in the court rolls of the manor. It has to be admitted that, apart from these two categories, the chances of establishing any detailed history for subordinate tenements are very poor. Detailed comparison of all maps and plans of the area, and especially of enclosure and tithe maps or detailed estate plans, affords the best hope of obtaining an approximate date of erection. The rates, being commonly paid by the employer in respect of the whole group of houses, are seldom useful and, to judge from cases where detailed documents do survive, changes of occupation were frequent. Surveys, and sale particulars for the whole estate or farm, occasionally offer scraps of information, but at widely separated dates. In most cases, after a preliminary inspection of the available evidence, it will have to be admitted that houses of this kind must be studied as examples of a type of dwelling rather than as individual buildings with histories.

(E) *Houses formed by conversion*
Much will depend in each case upon the period of conversion to a dwelling. In most instances the conversion is likely to have been modern, and the history of the building e.g. as a stable, barn, church, chapel, factory, warehouse, windmill or watermill really lies outside the limits of this study. Only when the change in use took place long ago will there be a domestic history of owners and occupiers to discover. The pattern of search will then conform for the

---

[36] The courts kept for Winchester College, originally in separate rolls for each manor, were recorded in two overlapping sets of books, 1557-1760 and 1585-1937. The minute books also survive for 1796-1877, 1882-1910. (Winchester College Muniments).

[37] For example there are many books of this kind, for single manors or groups, at Winchester College (e.g. Winchester College Muniments 23179-23199, covering c. 1630-c. 1850).

most part to that of one or other of the classes already discussed. A few special points deserve mention.

The history of barns, stables and other outbuildings must be sought as part of that of the houses to which they formerly belonged, and rather more attention than usual must be paid to the evidence of maps, plans and surveys of all kinds. Rates will only have been paid separately after the conversion to a dwelling. Factories and warehouses will presumably have been erected by industrial or commercial firms, and documentary evidence may well be found in business archives.[38] The conversion of mills is in rather a different category, since many mills have always had a house attached to them or standing close by, and their history is essentially that of a single tenement subsequently divided into two (the second part being the converted mill building). The legal status of mills, commonly belonging to the lords of manors or to the commonalty of corporate towns, implied that they were usually leasehold. Very many series of leases of city mills, and of mills belonging to corporate (ecclesiastical, collegiate, etc.) lords of manors survive, and their history can often be traced back to an early date, through several rebuildings on the same site. Care has to be exercised in identification, owing to the historical tendency of both windmills and watermills to be grouped near together, rather than to be built in isolation.[39]

[38] Consult the Business Archives Council, Dominion House, 37-45 Tooley Street, London, S.E.l.
[39] For mills see R. Wailes, *The English Windmill* (1954); *Tide Mills* (1957); I. Batten and D. Smith, *English Windmills*, 2 vols. (1930-32); L. Syson, *British Watermills* (1965).

PART II

ARCHITECTURAL EVIDENCE

In the first part of this study emphasis has been laid on the main sorts of documentary evidence which can be made to yield a history of named owners and occupiers of houses. This evidence from documents must not be considered in isolation, nor must it be given pre-eminence over the structural evidence to be derived directly from the fabric. It is a common error of historians to use the phrase 'there is no evidence' when what is meant is that there is no explicit *documentary* evidence. Yet it has been rightly held that, in any case where there is an irreconcilable confrontation between the evidence of structure and of documents, that derived from the fabric is to be preferred.[40] This dictum must, however, be interpreted in a strict sense: the conflict of evidence more often than not means that the document in question is not being correctly applied to the surviving building or detail. The late survival, for example, of Gothic detail in a remote part of the country does not invalidate documentation clearly showing erection on a hitherto clear site about 1700. On the other hand, the existence in England of explicitly Renaissance details will rule out any possibility whatever of such work being linked to a documented build[41] earlier than 1500.[42]

The first question to be asked in regard to architectural features concerns their authenticity. Is the surviving work original; if not, does it represent a careful copy of the old, or is it quite devoid of evidential value? To determine such questions by inspection of the fabric alone demands long experience and even then experts are fallible. A search should always be made for early photographs, and for drawings, sketches and paintings showing the building at any date. Photographs, especially if they are of known date and taken before a major documented repair, are generally the best possible evidence of original forms. All kinds of pre-photographic drawings, whether to scale or not, suffer both from deliberate artist's licence and from the inaccuracies of inadvertence. Careful comparison between graphic and photographic records is necessary, and will often establish a canon of authenticity in regard to a particular building or its details. The search for photographs and for drawings may in itself be a long one, involving both items in private possession at the

---

[40] See Francis Bond, 'On the comparative value of documentary and architectural evidence ...', *Journal of the Royal Institute of British Architects,* 26 November 1898, 17-35; W. A. Pantin, 'Monuments or Muniments', *Medieval Archaeology,* ii (1958), 158-68; and notably H. V. Molesworth Roberts, 'Historical Research in relation to Architecture', *Blackmansbury.* vii nos. 1 and 2 (1970), 3-8.

[41] The word 'build' is used of each of the parts of a building erected at any one time; i.e. unless it is all of one build.

[42] For the introduction of early Renaissance details see K. Harrison, *The Windows of King's College Chapel, Cambridge* (1952), 71-7; 'Notes on Sixteenth-century Ornament', *Journal of the British Society of Master Glass-Painters,* xi no. 3 (1953-54), 152-6; 'Katharine of Aragon's Pomegranate', *Transactions of the Cambridge Bibliographical Society,* ii no. 1 (1954), 88-92; A. P. Baggs, 'Sixteenth-century terra-cotta Tombs in East Anglia', *Archaeological Journal,* cxxv (1969). 297-301.

house itself or in the hands of former owners or occupiers and their descendants, and matter in various collections.[43]

The evidence to be derived from the actual structure is of several kinds. First of all may be considered formal date-stones incorporated in the building, with or without the names or initials of the building owners responsible. Although sound *prima facie* evidence of the date of the particular build or feature in which they are set, such tablets may have been brought from elsewhere or re-set after alterations. Names or initials must be checked against those of known owners and occupiers at the appropriate date, and any discrepancy thoroughly investigated. Rather less reliable as evidence are dates and initials on ornamental features and fittings: panelling, fireplaces, or stained glass. All these were very frequently moved from one building to another and the evidence has to be considered on its own merits in every case. Dated rainwater-heads are in a rather different category, since they have seldom been moved from one building to another. They are, however, in the stricter sense only evidence of their own date and, if provided with names, initials or heraldry, of the building patrons at the time. They are, nevertheless, often indicative of general rebuilding, of refronting, or of some major alteration. Great caution needs to be exercised in regard to dated heads since many were put up in accordance with the requirements of the Acts providing for adequate guttering, and local orders of enforcement.[44]

Evidential in quite a different way are fire insurance marks placed on the front of buildings. When each insurance company maintained its own brigade, these marks indicated the houses for which they were responsible, and the stamped number is that of the policy. It is to be regretted that very many marks have been removed to museums from surviving buildings, as well as from houses in course of demolition. This means that extensive search may be necessary to establish the provenance of an existing mark actually preserved locally. In cases where the mark is still on the building itself it leads in most cases directly to the books of the relevant insurance company. From the official record of the policy a great deal of information as to the house can be derived, and quite often the date of erection, since insurance was commonly effected as soon as the building was finished. The amount of specific detail given makes these policies outstandingly important among the earlier sources

[43] The principal collection of photographs is that of the National Monuments Record (Fortress House, Savile Row, London, W.1), and there are important local collections in many public libraries: that in the Birmingham Reference Library is regional in scope, and the Surrey County Council maintains a photographic record of antiquities, largely houses, within the boundaries of 1889-1965. The National Monuments Record also maintains indexes to photographs and to drawings in many other collections. For the very important series of drawings in the British Museum see C. E. Wright, *Archives*, iii no. 18 (1957), 78-87. The Victoria and Albert Museum (notably in its *loan* collection of paintings on temporary show in various galleries) has many topographical views, and its Library contains the best large collection of photographic postcards: these last are invaluable for information on alterations to houses during the past hundred years. Local art galleries and museums, and the regional museums service, should always be consulted. A good example of the bringing together of various types of graphic evidence is C. S. S. Higham, *Wimbledon Manor House under the Cecils* (1962).

[44] The Act of 11 Geo. I, c. 28, called for pipes on the sides or fronts of houses built in London and within the Bills of Mortality after 24 June 1725. In York an order was made 'pursuant to the Act of Parliament' on 2 May 1763 (York City Archives, M.17), which resulted in the addition to houses in the city of a large number of heads dated 1763 and 1764.

for building history.[45] In some cases the searcher will be able to obtain the information without recourse to the insurance company, since the original policies are sometimes found kept with the title deeds.

While this is not a treatise upon architectural history, a few hints may be given as to the kinds of evidence - apart from general style - which may be found in the study of historic houses in England. First to be considered is the main material of which the house is built: generally stone, brick, or timber-framing. Unusual materials include weather-boarding and the beaten earth types of walling such as cob.[46] The kinds of stone or brick used may, when considered in relation to the building history of the district as a whole, give very definite indications of approximate date.[47] Stonework should be specially examined for its type of tooling, and for the possible existence of masons' marks.[48] Both of these are specialized studies, and considerable caution is demanded of the observer, but they can be of great importance in some cases and as concurrent evidence leading towards a date which may be only one of several possibilities. Most masons' marks are personal signs indicating the actual man who hewed the stone, and showing his responsibility for any imperfections. No early registers of marks have survived, though a few are identifiable because used alongside signatures on documents. In general they can only be considered strongly indicative of date when several *relatively unusual* marks are found associated on more than one building. Marks of clearly numerical significance are evidence that the stones were cut at the quarry according to a drawing or set of written instructions, and numbered for erection in their correct courses. At the Portland quarries, special numeral marks indicated the contents of each block in cubic feet.

Brick made of local clays in former times varied very greatly in colour and texture, and the sizes of bricks were not completely standardized until relatively modern times.[49] Search for similar examples of brickwork in the same district may reveal a dated building, and it is also worthwhile searching the churchyards for brick box-tombs which can be fairly closely dated from their inscriptions. Occasionally the bricklayers scratched names or initials,

[45] For fire insurance marks and records see L. M. Wulcko, *Amateur Historian*, ix no. 1, 3-8; and J. H. Thomas, *History*, liii no. 179, 381-4.

[46] For materials generally see N. Davey, *A History of Building Materials* (1961); A. Clifton-Taylor, *The Pattern of English Building* (3rd ed., 1972). On separate materials: N. Lloyd, *A History of English Brickwork* (1925); A. R. Warnes, *Building Stones* (1926); W. J. Arkell, *Oxford Stone* (1947); F. H. Crossley, *Timber Building in England* (1951). For the interrelation between materials and methods see C. F. Innocent, *The Development of English Building Construction* (1916/1971); and L. F. Salzman, *Building in England down to 1540* (1952/1967).

[47] The chapters on quarrying in the Industries section of many of the Victoria County Histories are of outstanding importance in regard to local supplies of stone at various dates.

[48] For tooling of mediaeval date the standard study is that of E. S. Prior in *Proceedings of the Harrow Architectural Club*, 1904. There are modern studies of masons' marks by R. H. C. Davis, 'A Catalogue of Masons' Marks as an aid to Architectural History', *Journal of the British Archaeological Association* (3rd series, xvii, 1954), 43-76; by K. Wilson in *Amateur Historian*, ii no. 8, 232-4; and by F. W. Brooks, *Masons' Marks* (East Yorkshire Local History Society, Local History Series no. 1, 1961). For the quarry marks used on Portland stone see T. B. Groves in *Proceedings of the Dorset Natural History and Archaeological Field Club*, xv (1894).

[49] Plain roofing tiles had been standardized by an Act of 1477 (17 Edw. IV, c. 3, 4). Tables showing the sizes of dated examples of brick are given by Lloyd (see above, note 46); and for early brickwork see J. A. Wight, *Brick Building in England from the Middle Ages to 1550* (1972). Bricks of exceptionally large size were commonly used in the period of the tax on bricks, levied by number, from 1784 to 1850.

and dates, on soft brickwork of fine quality, and the red 'rubber' bricks of quoins and window arches should be carefully examined for such graffiti. Glaziers likewise sometimes marked window panes with names and dates written very small with a diamond, and plumbers cast names and dates on the lead sheets used for roofs and gutters. In such cases care must be taken to note whether the inscription is cast on the original sheet, or is only a piece cut out and soldered on at a more modern renewal. It has to be borne in mind that most roofing materials need relaying in about one to two hundred years.

The various types of timber-framing and of roof-trusses form a highly specialized and still controversial study. Undue reliance should not be placed upon precise dates suggested unless these are supported by scientifically prepared dendrochronological evidence (based on the correlation of widths of annual rings accurately measured, with meteorological records of weather in past times).[50] Variations in types of structure are in part regional, in part chronological, and have to be studied in the light of many buildings within a given area.[51] Timber-framing in general should not be termed 'half-timbering', but the special kind of framing in which broad vertical posts are separated by narrow strips of infilling of approximately equal width indicates a date of construction after about 1475, and probably within the next hundred years. The infilling of most timber frames was originally of wattle-and-daub; where brick is found it is usually a later replacement. Approximate dating of the brickwork will yield the period of repair, not of erection.

Finally a word should be added on the subject of mouldings. From the twelfth to the early sixteenth century the precise forms of mouldings were drawn to full-size by the master craftsmen, and cut accordingly by their subordinates. The profiles used indicate not only the approximate period but, in many cases, the highly characteristic work of individual architects and their immediate pupils. Along with window-tracery, mouldings provide the main stylistic key to the architecture of the Middle Ages. Mouldings cut in timber more often than not lag behind the style set by the principal stonemason architects, and are thus less clearly indicative of date. Along with details of framing and jointing they do give general suggestions of period. Comparatively little reliance should be placed on the much more stereotyped mouldings of the Renaissance period after c. 1550, and other characteristics are a more trustworthy guide.[52]

[50] Pioneer studies of English dendrochronology are A. W. G. Lowther, 'Dendrochronology' in *The Archaeological News Letter*, no. 11 (March 1949), 1-3; 'The Date of timbers from ... Chilcomb Church and ... the River Hamble', in *Papers and Proceedings of the Hampshire Field Club and Archaeological Society*, xvii part 2 (1951), 130-3; D. J. Schove and A. W. G. Lowther, 'Tree-Rings and Medieval Archaeology' in *Medieval Archaeology*, i (1957), 78-95. It should be noted that dating by radio-carbon methods yields only very approximate dates and is exceptionally liable to be upset by contamination; it has therefore little relevance to English architectural history.

[51] For a bibliography of the subject see R. de Z. Hall, ed., *A Bibliography on Vernacular Architecture* (1972). The best general work is M. Wood, *The English Mediaeval House* (1965).

[52] A handy guide to mediaeval mouldings is H. Forrester, *Medieval Gothic Mouldings* (1972).

PART III

THE HISTORICAL BACKGROUND

In so far as any given search for the history of a house may have been successful, it will provide a more or less complete skeleton of facts about the house, and the mere names of its former owners and occupiers. Except as an exercise in research, or as part of a study in the dating of local architecture, such a result has little value. A great deal more needs to be done to clothe the skeleton with flesh and transform the bare tabulation into living social history. The architectural historian must transform himself into genealogist and biographer in order to get the full value out of the work already done.

Though here dealt with separately as a matter of convenience and to avoid confusing the student, the two aspects of research should, ideally, be carried on side by side at the same time. As names of former owners and occupiers, and perhaps of architects and builders too, come to light, they should be formed into an alphabetical index. No name, however apparently obscure, should be omitted. As time goes on, facts should be accumulated upon each and every name, so far as possible. The searcher should set no limits, for he cannot know what facts may be relevant: his best guide is that offered by Austin Freeman's great detective, Dr. Thorndyke: 'When I am gravelled for lack of evidence, (I) collect indiscriminately all the information that I can obtain that is in the remotest way connected with the problem ...'[53] By such methods a pool of information will be obtained, and out of it interesting historical figures will emerge.

The sources to be used will vary according to the locality: in a city or large town there is a good chance that former owners, and perhaps occupiers too, may have acquired local if not national fame. It is always worth looking for names in the *Dictionary of National Biography,* using first the *Index and Epitome,* but both printed and manuscript collections on county or civic worthies will be more generally rewarding. For many areas there is likely to be a book or article on local literary associations, and there should be much ready-made information in any place where there is a flourishing local antiquarian body. For the middle of the nineteenth century the accessible Census Returns (1841, 1851, 1861) provide a detailed picture of the family occupying any and every home.[54] The information given by the Census as to occupations offers fresh clues, as do the casual and sporadic descriptions found in deeds and other records. This aspect of social life can be traced further back through the printed directories, for London effectively to about 1750 and in the country generally to the 1780s.[55] For the more substantial

---

[53] R. Austin Freeman, *As a Thief in the Night* (1928/1971), chap. viii, p. 136.

[54] The census returns can be consulted at the Public Record Office; many local record offices and public libraries have photocopies of the returns for their own respective areas. See L. C. Hector in *Amateur Historian,* i no. 6, 174-7; and M. Beresford, *ibid.,* v no. 8, 260-9.

[55] See C. W. F. Goss, *The London Directories, 1677-1855* (1932); and J. E. Norton, *Guide to the National and Provincial Directories of England and Wales, excluding London, ... before 1856* (Royal Historical Society, Guides and Handbooks no. 5, 1950). The Guildhall Library, London, is the best place for serious work on a full range of directories (for the country at large as well as for London). There is also an important collection in the library of the Society of Genealogists (see below, note 56).

members of society, likely to be voters, there is also the very valuable body of information to be derived from Poll Books. Many were printed and others survive as isolated manuscripts, usually in local libraries.[56] The amount of information given varies, but some books include occupation and residential address as well as the place of a qualifying freehold; they are especially valuable because they give the addresses of qualified voters in one county or city who happened to live in distant places, and thus provide a proof of identity otherwise hard to find.

The basic sources for the genealogist, concerned with the history of a given family of owners or occupiers, are parish registers (back to 1538 in favourable cases, generally to about 1600) and wills (generally available to the late fourteenth century, but in some cases, as London, still earlier).[57] The problems of jurisdictions and peculiars cannot be dealt with here, but the searcher will always be able to get adequate assistance over such technicalities from the staff of local record offices. Associated with wills are Probate Inventories, which can be immensely informative, but were all too often excused, and have in any case been entirely lost for many of the courts of probate. Search should, however, be made for the will and inventory of every known occupier of a house (down to c. 1800, when the inventories cease altogether), as few other sources can give so detailed a picture of the separate rooms and outbuildings and their contents[58] (see Appendix G). Another source for very detailed information on individual buildings which, in the mid-seventeenth century, belonged to the Crown or to the Church, is the series of Parliamentary Surveys, now in a number of places of deposit.[59]

Two other sources of outstanding importance are monuments and gravestones, and the advertisements in local newspapers. Although as a general rule surviving monuments commemorate the wealthier members of the community, this is by no means always the case, and an immense body of social as well as personal history can be drawn from thorough study of the tablets and stones in the neighbouring churches, chapels, graveyards and

---

[56] For poll books see J. Cannon in *History*, xlvii no. 160, 166-9; J. M. Sims, ed., *A Catalogue of Directories and Poll Books in the possession of the Society of Genealogists* (Society of Genealogists, 1964).

[57] A parish register may have been printed, or a manuscript or typescript copy be available. The two complementary lists issued by the Society of Genealogists: *Parish Register Copies*, I: Society of Genealogists Collection (3rd ed., 1970); II: Other than the Society of Genealogists Collection (1971) give the general position and this can be brought up to date by inquiry at the local public library. The original registers may have been deposited in the diocesan record office, but many remain in the custody of the incumbents. In some regions (notably for the ancient diocese of York) there are well preserved series of Bishop's Transcripts - contemporary copies of the registers of baptisms, marriages and burials submitted annually from each parish. These can usually be consulted at diocesan record offices.
The guide to wills is A. Camp, *Wills and their Whereabouts* (Society of Genealogists, 1963), but it is also useful to consult the original work by B. G. Bouwens (1939) on which this is based. It should be noted that the wills, administrations and inventories of the Prerogative Court of Canterbury are now at the Public Record Office and can be consulted in the separate probate search room. On wills see also R. Sharpe France in *History*, I no. 168, 36-9; and note 23 above. For valuable hints on wills, inventories and other classes of records inadequately used see Joan Thirsk, 'Unexplored Sources in Local Records', *Archives*, vi no. 29 (1963), 8-12.

[58] For inventories see F. W. Steer, *Farm and Cottage Inventories of Mid-Essex* (Chelmsford, Essex Record Office, 1950); and in *History*, xlvii no. 161, 287-90; also B. C. Jones in *Amateur Historian*, ii no. 3, 76-9.

[59] For the Parliamentary Surveys see S. C. Newton in *History*, liii no. 177, 51-4; and Appendix E(1) below.

cemeteries.[60] A vandalistic fashion of removing gravestones from churchyards has gained ground in recent years, and is to be deplored by all students of local and family history. It is to be noted that provision is generally made for a record of all legible inscriptions to be preserved before clearance, and this should be deposited in the diocesan record office. Many other collections of the monumental inscriptions at particular places exist in the library of the Society of Genealogists.[61]

Advertisements in newspapers offer an enormous field of work to the diligent student with ample time. They cover the period from about 1725 to the present day, and the volume of material since 1800 is generally too vast for specific search unless an index has been compiled (as for example by the public libraries at Birmingham and York). The relatively small papers of the eighteenth century, mostly issued only once or twice a week, are easier to tackle, and can give a heavy yield of rich detail for the time spent on them. Advertisements of houses to be let or sold, of businesses carried on at stated addresses, and biographical information of all kinds will be found besides, in the news columns, references to births, marriages and deaths in many local families, not all socially prominent. Notices of change of address are not infrequent, and can be extremely useful as a supplement to or substitute for the entries in rate books. Though covering only a limited period, the newspapers as a printed source commonly accessible at public libraries are particularly suitable for the amateur in research; but to get the best out of them does demand patience and application.[62]

As a final work, albeit of supererogation, an attempt may be made to follow up the architects, builders and craftsmen who have been concerned with the erection, alteration and repairs of houses studied. An important basic distinction to be kept in mind is that between the creatively designed work of architecture, and the traditional building. Only the former will have involved the employment of an architect, though he may in earlier periods have been described as a master mason, bricklayer or carpenter. Architects in many cases will have been brought from a distance; most of the actual building craftsmen will have been local men, and very likely responsible for whole streets, terraces or groups of houses as well as those individually scattered through a district. There is a tendency for certain trades to run in families, and it is likely that local dynasties of builders, plasterers, plumbers, and painters and others will be found. In some cases they may have themselves occupied the

---

[60] See F. Burgess, *English Churchyard Memorials* (1963), and a wide range of general and local books and articles on monuments and epitaphs. York, for example, is covered by two modern books by J. B. Morrell, *York Monuments* (n.d.), and *The Biography of the Common Man of the City of York as recorded in his Epitaph* (1947); and there is a combined alphabetical list of inscriptions in all the parish churches to 1788 in the condensation of *Eboracum* (York, T. Wilson and R. Spence, 1788), ii, 188-250.

[61] The library of the Society of Genealogists is at 37 Harrington Gardens, London, S.W.7. It may be used by non-members on payment of a fee.

[62] For newspapers see G. R. Mellor in *Amateur Historian,* ii no. 4, 97-101; The Times, *Tercentenary Handlist of English and Welsh Newspapers, Magazines and Reviews* (1920); R. S. Crane, F. B. Kaye and M. E. Prior, *A Census of British Newspapers and Periodicals 1620-1800* (University of North Carolina Press, 1927); G. A. Cranfield, *A Hand-List of English Provincial Newspapers and Periodicals 1700-1760* (Cambridge Bibliographical Society, 1952); 'Additions and Corrections ...' in *Transactions of the Cambridge Bibliographical Society,* ii (1956), 269-74; R. M. Wiles, 'Further Additions and Corrections ...', *ibid.,* ii (1958), 385-9; *Freshest Advices, Early Provincial Newspapers in England* (Ohio State University Press, 1965).

house whose history is being studied; but in all cases the discovery of other houses made by the same hands is likely to supply comparative information on the structure, and to enable lost features to be reconstructed in imagination.[63]

[63] See H. V. Molesworth Roberts, 'Notes on some English Architects', *Blackmansbury*, vii nos. 1 and 2 (1970), 9-25. Some specialized studies of buildings are: on Farms, by E. J. T. Collins in *Archives*, vii no. 35 (1966), 143-9; on Inns, by W. B. Johnson in *Amateur Historian*, vi no. 1, 18-21; and by W. E. Tate, *ibid.*, viii no. 4, 126-30; on Town History by E. M. Halcrow in *Amateur Historian*, i no. 10, 308-11; and on Suburbs by H. J. Dyos, *ibid.*, iv no. 7, 275-81.

APPENDIX OF DOCUMENTS

This appendix includes examples of documents of seven main kinds, outstandingly useful for the history of houses. Examples of many other types of record will be found in the specialized articles referred to in the footnotes, particularly those in *History* (from volume xlvii onwards) which constitute a series of Short Guides to Records under the general editorship of L. M. Munby, also re-issued as a separate volume (1972); and of ecclesiastical records - particularly puzzling to the amateur - in D. M. Owen, *The Records of the Established Church in England* (British Records Association, Archives and the User no. 1, 1970). Study of the examples of documents included, with photographs of the originals and transcriptions, in guides to palaeography such as Emmison (see above, note 1) and H. Grieve, *Examples of English Handwriting, 1150-1750* (Essex County Council, 2nd ed., 1959) will also familiarize the student with much of the material he will meet.

APPENDIX A

RATE BOOKS

The example chosen is taken from the well preserved series of rating assessments, starting in 1774, for the York parish of Holy Trinity, Micklegate (now deposited in the Borthwick Institute, York). Assessments covering the ten years 1822-23 to 1832-33 are shown with parallel extracts from the directories of York published in 1823 and 1830, the latter being the first directory to show street numbering in the relevant area. The block of houses shown is on the south-east side of Blossom Street, outside Micklegate Bar, and runs from the corner of Nunnery Lane (i.e. from the Nunnery or Bar Convent, now no. 17) as far as the Lion and Lamb, an inn which has existed on the same site through the whole of the last two centuries. Another fixed point within the block is shown, the entry which first appeared as Park's Passage in 1828 and which survived as St. Mary's Court until 1939, between the present nos. 29 and 31.

It will be seen that modern numbers have not been assigned to all the properties assessed. This is partly due to rebuilding at later dates combined with alterations in the total number of properties, but also indicates some degree of uncertainty in identification. The modern no. 37 has never corresponded to any building on the street frontage. It should be noted that the additional entries in the assessments for land, gardens, etc. do not necessarily relate to property adjacent to the houses on which the principal assessments were raised. The word 'Moat' indicates occupation of part of the old City Ditch on the other side of Nunnery Lane. The entries have here been tabulated from south-west to north-east, contrary to the run of the present numbers, in order to preserve the evidential value of the succession in the original assessments.

To reach the results here shown it was necessary to tabulate the rating assessments from 1774 to 1854 and the directories and electoral rolls from 1823 to 1963, and also to collate the information with evidence from other sources, notably the Ordnance Survey plan of York on the scale of 5 feet to 1 mile, surveyed in 1851 and published in 1853. Complexities of street numbering were revealed in the process: in 1830 a consecutive numbering started outside Micklegate Bar on the north-west side of the street, running as far as no. 26 at the angle of the Holgate Road; crossing Blossom Street the numbers returned from no. 27 (the then Sun Inn) along the south-east side of the street back to the Bar. According to this system the Lion and Lamb was no. 36 and the Bar Convent (not numbered) notionally no. 46. In 1868 the numbering was changed throughout and two numbers were eliminated, so that the Lion and Lamb became no. 34 and the Bar Convent no. 44; this numbering appeared consistently until 1909. In 1910 a more radical change took place, the street being numbered outwards from the Bar on both sides, the odd numbers running along the south-east (left-hand) side of the street. The numbers of the block here shown begin with the Bar Convent as no. 17 and include the notional no. 37 for premises behind the frontage no. 35; the total of numbers allocated to the block was thus increased by one, from eleven to twelve.

Although the rating assessments are mostly well written, a considerable amount of inconsistency in spelling occurs, and is at times in serious conflict with the printed directories. Neither authority can be accepted: external evidence shows that 'Cropper' of the directory is right for the 1830 licensee of the Lion and Lamb, as against the 'Crappen' of the rate. On the other hand, the locally famous William Hotham, alderman from 1792 and Lord Mayor of York in 1802 and 1819 (died 8 August 1836) is incorrectly printed as 'Holmes'. After Hotham's death the house, which had belonged to the Bar Convent since 1781, was converted to become a residence for the chaplain (Royal Commission on Historical Monuments, *City of York,* iii, 1972, 63) and disappeared as a separate assessment from the rates. The adjacent house to the south-west (modern no. 21) was in part a new building of 1845 and was for many years the home of George Leeman, M.P. (1809-1882). In its predecessor lived, as shown by this extract, the noted Quaker missionary, botanist and nurseryman James Backhouse (1794-1869), from 1824 until 1831, when he left York on his ten-year missionary journey to Australia and South Africa. The very wide social range of the occupants of this small block is noteworthy, but typical of the historic pattern of the York community.

Modern Nos.	Rate 1822-1823		Baines's York Directory 1823	Rate 1823-1824	
(39)	John Richardson	£6. 5. 0	John Richardson, victualler Lion and Lamb, Blossom St.	John Richardson	
(35)	John Steward	£4.10. 0	Steward, G. and Sons, combs, lanthorn light and drinking horn manufacturers*	John Steward	
(33)	" late Healey	£1. 0. 0			
(31)	John Wilberfoss	£4.15. 0	Wilberforce, John, cowkeeper	John Wilberfoss	
(29)	Mrs. Kirk	£5. 0. 0	Kirk, Mrs. Mary	Mrs. Kirk	
(27)	Mrs. Wakeman	£7.10. 0		Mrs. Solving	
				Mrs. Hutchinson	£3. 5. 0
(21)			Smith, Mrs. Mary	late Mrs. Smith	£3. 5. 0
(19)	Wm. Hotham, esq.	£10. 0. 0	Hotham, William, Esq., Alderman	Wm. Hotham. esq.	£10. 0. 0
	" Moat	£1.11. 8		" "for land	£1.11. 8
(17)	Mrs. Coyney	£37.10. 0	Coyney, Mrs. Elizabeth, governess of the Convent (Rev. Mother Superior) Rev. James Newsham, officiating clergyman	Mrs. Coyney	

*In the church of St. Mary Bishophill Junior, south aisle, is a monument to George Steward, comb manufacturer, died 1820, his wife Elizabeth, 1833, and children

Modern Nos.	Rate 1824-1825	Rate 1825-1826	Rate 1828-1829
(39)	Mr. J. Richardson	Mr. Richardson £6. 5. 0	Mr. Richardson £8. 0. 0
(35)	Mrs. Steward	Mr. Steward £4.10. 0	Mr. Steward £4.10. 0
(31)	Mr. J. Wilberfoss	Mr. J. Wilberfoss £4.15. 0	Mr. Park, house and tenements £6. 0. 0
			(PARK'S PASSAGE)
(29)	Mrs. Kirk	Mrs. Kirk £5. 0. 0	Mrs. Kirk £5. 0. 0
(27)	Mrs. Solving	Mrs. Salvin £7.10. 0	Mrs. Salvin £7.10. 0
	Mrs. Hutchinson £10. 0. 0	Mrs. Hutchinson £10. 0. 0	Mr. Hutchinson £12. 0. 0
(21)	Mr. Jo. Backhouse £10. 0. 0 " " garden £3. 0. 0	Mr. Jo. Backhouse £10. 0. 0 " " garden £3. 0. 0	Mr. Backhouse £12. 0. 0 " " garden £3. 0. 0
(19)	Wm. Hotham, esq. £10. 0. 0 " " for Moat £1.11. 8	Wm. Hotham, esq. £10. 0. 0 " " for Moat £1.11. 6	Mr. Hotham £10. 0. 0 " " " Moat £1.11. 6
(17)	Mrs. Coyney	Mrs. Coyney £37.10. 0	Mrs. Coyney £37.10. 0

Modern Nos.	1830 Nos.	1830 York Directory	Rate 1830-1831		Rate 1832-1833	
(39)	36	Wm. Cropper, victualler Lion and Lamb	Mr. Crappen	£8. 0. 0	Mr. Bell (Thomas)	£8. 0. 0
(35)	37	Steward, G. and Sons, comb manufacturers	Mr. Steward	£4.10. 0	Mr. Steward (G.)	£5. 0. 0
	38	Steward, Mrs. Eliz.				
(31)	39	Park, Alex., joiner &c.	Mr. Park, ho. & tenements	£6. 0. 0	Mr. Park (Alex.), Ho. & tenements	£6. 0. 0
		(PARK'S PASSAGE) at 40 Blossom Street	later		ST. MARY'S COURT	
	40	Richardson, Wm., shoemaker				
(29)	41	Kirk, Mrs. Mary	Mrs. Kirk	£5. 0. 0	Mrs. Kirk (Mary)	£5. 0. 0
(27)	42	Salvin, Miss Eliz.	Mrs. Salvin	£7.10. 0	Mrs. Salvin	£7.10. 0
(25)	43	Hutchinson, Rev. Cyril George	Mr. Hutchinson	£12. 0. 0	The Rev. Mr. Hutchinson	£12. 0. 0
(21)	44	Backhouse, Jas. (seedsman)	Mr. Backhouse " garden	£12. 0. 0 £3. 0. 0	Thos. Barstow, esq. " garden	£12. 0. 0 £3. 0. 0
(19)	45	Holmes, Wm., Ald.	Mr. Hotham " Moat	£10. 0. 0 £1.11. 6	Ald. Hotham (Wm.) " Moat	£10. 0. 0 £1.11. 6
(17)		Newsham, Rev. James Bar Convent	Mrs. Coyney	£37.10. 0	Nunnery House	£37.10. 0

APPENDIX B

DEEDS

Most deeds, other than those of the Middle Ages, are of inordinate length and unsuitable for quotation in full. The items given below are abstracts from the memorials of deeds enrolled before the Lord Mayor of York, and relate to some of the properties in the block in Blossom Street dealt with in Appendix A.

(1) Two deeds concerning the Lion and Lamb Inn, shown by the Rate Assessments to have been occupied by Thomas Sellers or Sellar until 1784, by Mrs. Sellar in 1785-91, and later by Mr. Bentley, who is identified by the second deed as Robert Bentley (York City Archives, E. 95, ff. 128v, 148v).

(a) Indenture of Mortgage dated 26 November 1792 and enrolled 27 November between Richard Jackson yeoman and his wife Elizabeth of the first part and Rachael Seller widow of the second part: concerning a Messuage used as an Inn out of Micklegate Bar on the south-east side of the street with Stables Outbuildings and Yard late in the occupation of the said Rachael Seller and now of the said Richard Jackson; and a Garth Orchard Croft or Close and Garden behind late in the occupation of Robert Nutbrown and now of the said Richard Jackson; also a Workshop or Shed and Chambers over it adjoining now in the occupation of Vincent Sancton blacksmith.
Mortgage for 1000 years for £250 and interest at 4½%.

(b) Lease and Release dated 31 August and 1 September 1794 and enrolled on 1 September the lease between Richard Jackson yeoman of the first part and William Jackson of Streethouses in Steeton in the County of the City of York yeoman and Thomas Todd of Steeton yeoman of the second part; and the release between Richard Jackson and his wife Elizabeth (1) and the said William Jackson and Thomas Todd (2):
concerning a Messuage (described as above) late in the occupation of Rachael Seller widow since of the said Richard Jackson and now of Robert Bentley; and a Garth etc. behind late in the occupation of Robert Nutbrown since of Richard Jackson and now of the said Robert Bentley; also a Workshop etc. now or late in the occupation of Vincent Sancton blacksmith with half of a Well etc.
Conveyance on trust to sell and pay off the Mortgage to Mrs. Seller.

Robert Nutbrown (c. 1754-1830) was a market gardener who, in addition to this ground outside the walls, was lessee from 1785 to 1811 of the important Trinity Gardens off Micklegate, the former precinct of Holy Trinity Priory. He took up the Freedom of York in 1793 but was in gaol for debt in 1814 and died in March 1830 (*York Courant* 3 Jan 1814; *Yorkshire Gazette* 27 March 1830).

(2) Four deeds concerning the property adjacent on the south-west to the Bar Convent, including the modern no. 19. The first three deeds carry the story of this property back to a date substantially earlier than the start of the

surviving Rate Assessments, which show William Green esq. as occupier in 1774-81 of (no. 19), and 'Mr. Santon' beyond him to the south-west in 1779-80. (York City Archives, E. 93, ff. 244, 246; E. 94, ff. 140, 235).

(a)   Lease and Release dated 8 and 9 October 1750 and enrolled on 12 October the lease between Francis Jefferson esq. only son and heir and executor of Edward Jefferson grocer deceased; John Benson gent. and his wife Faith; Mary Baxter of Little Ponton in the County of Lincoln widow; Ann Geldart spinster and Hannah Geldart spinster (which Faith Mary Ann and Hannah are the daughters and coheiresses of Faith Geldart late of York widow deceased) (1) and William Smith out of Micklegate Bar gent. (2); and the release between Francis Jefferson (1); the said John Benson and his wife Faith (and others) (2) and the said William Smith (3):
concerning a Messuage with a Brewhouse etc. without Micklegate Bar on the south-east side of the street the Nunnery next on the north-east; an Orchard or Frontstead where a house formerly stood now a garden belonging to the said John Benson and his wife Faith etc. and now in possession of Samuel Smith gardener on the south-west late in the possession of — Mennell esq. now of William Thornton and also all that said piece of ground called an Orchard or Frontstead containing two acres next to the above messuage on the south-west and on the back part thereof with a Stable and Garden house now in the possession of Samuel Smith gardener; also a little Paddock also out of Micklegate Bar adjoining upon York Field with land below it lying open to York Field now or late in the possession of William Windhouse and Mr. Green
(also another messuage on the opposite side of the street near the Mount) all which Messuages etc. were heretofore the estate of William Pemberton deceased afterwards of Ann Pemberton deceased his daughter and heiress and were by her devised to the said Faith Geldart deceased.
Absolute conveyance for £551.

(b)   Lease and release by way of Mortgage dated 14 and 15 October 1750 and enrolled on 14 October the lease between William Smith out of Micklegate Bar gent. (1) and Mary Girdler widow (2); and the release between William Smith and his wife Esther (1) and Mary Girdler widow (2):
concerning a Messuage with a Brewhouse (etc. all as described above; also the messuage on the north-west side of the street; and also a messuage in North Street in the City of York).
Mortgage for £400.

(c)   Lease and Release dated 13 and 14 May 1773 and enrolled on 14 May 1773 the lease between Thomas Swann merchant and William Smith gent. (1); William Greene of Thundercliffe Grange in the parish of Ecclesfield and County of York esq. (2); and the release between Thomas Swann (1); William Smith and his wife Esther (2) and William Greene (3):
concerning a Messuage with a Brewhouse Garden etc. without Micklegate Bar on the south-east side of the street (as above) and the Orchard on the south-west side and south-east end and the premises late in the possession of Samuel Smith and now of John Roebuck and the said William Smith all which were

some time ago in the possession of — Meynell esq. afterwards of William Thornton since in the possession of Mrs. Ann Aspinall and late untenanted but now in the occupation of the said William Greene.
Absolute conveyance for £500.

(d)   Lease and Release dated 1 and 2 November 1781 and enrolled on 12 November the lease between William Greene of the suburbs of the City of York esq. (1); Ann Aspinall of the suburbs of the City of York spinster (2); and the release between William Greene and his wife Hannah (1) and Ann Aspinall (2):
concerning a Messuage in which the said William Greene now lives with a Kitchen Brewhouse Outhouses Edifices New Erections Yard Garden etc. without Micklegate Bar in the suburbs on the south-east side of the Street - the Nunnery next on north-east and a house garden and orchard on the south-west and adjoining now or late in the several occupations of Vincent Sancton and John Roebuck with Heirlooms.
Absolute conveyance for £840.

Vincent Sancton was a blacksmith (above, deeds 1.a and b) who was tenant of a workshop next the Lion and Lamb as well as of part of this property next to (no. 19) Blossom Street. John Roebuck was one of a family of York gardeners and fruiterers who occupied various gardens around the city. For Samuel Smith see Appendix C (2), below.

(3)   Two deeds of Mortgage concerning property adjoining the Lion and Lamb Inn on the south-west, shown by the Rate Assessments to have been occupied as a house and garden ground by George Hayton in 1774 and until 1791 (York City Archives, E. 94, ff. 61, 158).
The mortgage, for £150 and interest in 1764, had grown to £210 only ten years later, and in 1779 (when it was transferred by a further deed, ibid., f. 212) to £240.

(a)   Lease and Release by way of Mortgage dated 20 and 21 August 1764 and enrolled on 21 August the lease between Hannah Sowden widow; George Hayton gardener and Thomas Seller yeoman and his wife Rachel (1); Elizabeth Agar spinster (2); and the release between Hannah Sowden (1); George Hayton (2); Thomas Seller and his wife Rachel (3) and Elizabeth Agar (4):
concerning a Messuage now let into several tenements with Stable and a large Garth Orchard Croft or Close and Garden on the back without Micklegate Bar adjoining on a Close of Mr. Robert Bewlay's on the west and a messuage of Mr. Girdler in possession of the said Hannah Sowden on the east all late the estate of Mary Cobb deceased.
Mortgage for £150 and interest.

(b)   Lease and Release by way of Mortgage dated 22 and 23 June 1774 and enrolled on 21 June 1774 (sic) the lease between Thomas Seller innholder and his wife Rachel and Seth Agar of Pocklington in the County of York gent. (1); John Redhead gent. (2); and the release between Thomas Seller and his wife

Rachel (1); Seth Agar (2); Jane Allanson spinster (3); and the said John Readhead (4):
concerning a Messuage (described as above).
Mortgage for £210.

When the mortgage was transferred on 17 July 1779 the adjoining messuage on the (north-)east was stated to be in the possession of the said Thomas Seller and his undertenants (i.e. the Lion and Lamb property) and the mortgaged premises included a Workshop and Shed lately erected in the said Garth now occupied by Vincent Sandon (read Sancton) blacksmith. The premises thereafter formed part of the property associated with the Lion and Lamb (in the deeds 1.a and b above). George Hayton was admitted to the freedom of the city of York in 1776 as a seedsman and gardener; in 1779 he was described as of the suburbs of York (York City Archives, D.14, p 198) and in 1784 as of Blossom Street (Poll Book). In 1782 he had been elected a Councillor for Micklegate Ward, but in February 1790 he was trying to sell his business 'at a house and garden situate without Micklegate Bar' and in January 1791 advertised that he was selling up because of ill-health; his death at the age of 72 was reported in November (*Yorkshire Herald,* 13 Feb 1790; 29 Jan and 12 Nov 1791). For his will and inventory see Appendix C (1) below.

APPENDIX C

WILLS

Wills and probate Inventories (see also Appendix G below) are closely associated, but for practical purposes convey quite different types of information. It is comparatively rare for a will to describe house property in detail, whereas a corresponding inventory will list each room with its contents. On the other hand it is quite largely from wills that the descent of houses and land, as well as the relationships of successive owners, can be traced. In the first example below a very short will is followed by a detailed inventory. They have been kept together and presented here as they continue the story of the gardener George Hayton (above, Appendix B.3).

(1)   Will and Inventory of George Hayton late of the parish of Holy Trinity Micklegate without Micklegate Barr in the Suburbs of the City of York Gardener (Borthwick Institute, York: York Wills, December 1791).

(a)   Will dated 31 October 1791 leaving all estate and effects to my Housekeeper Mary Smith; she to be sole Executrix.
the Mark and Seal of George X Hayton
Witnesses: William Colbord   William Watson   John Harger
Past (i.e. proved) 22 December 1791   over £20 (in value of the personalty)

(b)   Schedule and Valuation of Household Furniture &c. ... at his House without Micklegate Barr York   Dec. 1 1791   by Matthew Browne Appraiser

Kitchen Range,   Jack,   Spitt saw & prickers   2 Iron Candlesticks fender   shovell   Tongs   poker   sett small fire Irons   hanging Iron Beef fork   Stake tongs   4 Iron skewers   Tin Box & Esr.   (? Tinder Box & Extinguisher)   plait Cover   6 Brass Candlesticks   2 brass Ladels   pot cover & skimer   Coper Can Cofie   2 Coper Covers   Brass warming pan Bellows & Lanthorn   Wood Desk   a 24 Hours Clock   deel Table   Wood Horse   a round Table & old sqr. Do.   Coach seat   wood stool   salt pot   an arm'd Chair   3 old Chairs   Cofie Mill   Tea Chest   Iron Stand Oak Desk   Old looking Glass   Corner Cupboard   Trelis petition to Bedstead   Bed   bolster   2 pillows & Old beding   7 pictures   20 Earthan plaits   2 delph Bowles   stand for flowers   3 Cups & Saucrs   a Bason Dresser & Cratch Bird Cage   old Table

Pantry

Tin   Oven   Cullender   Cheese toaster   Tea Kettle   Coper Can   1 Spit driping pan   4 Knives & Forks   Mortaer & pestill   Cleaver   Frying Pan Brass pan   1 Chair   30 pots different Sorts

Back Kitchen

Meat sconce   Close (Clothes) Horse   Dry ruber   2 Vashetts   Churn   a Table 2 Bowls   a Chair   a close stool   2 Washing Tubs   2 Water Tubs Tool Chest   a block   1 Old Table

Parlour

Bedstead   dining Table & round Do.   6 Matted Chairs   1 Corner Chair Corner Cupboard   a looking Glass   Range   2 Brass Arms & Tea Tray 10 pictures   few Cups & Sawcrs

Up Stairs

Bedstead & hangings   Bed & Bedding   6 Old Chairs   old Table   Bedstead & hangings   2 old Chest drawers   a silver Watch   silver Cup & sauce boat   2 pr. Sheets   2 Pr. slips   3 Table Cloths   3 Towells   pump   2 hot bed frames   3 Barrows   a few work Tools   10 hand Glasses brok & Stock in Garden

£28.11.0

Hayton's housekeeper and legatee Mary Smith may have been identical with the Mrs. Mary Smith occupying the site of (no. 21) Blossom Street in 1823 (Appendix A, above), but this seems rather unlikely in view of the lapse of over 30 years. On the other hand, Hayton's holdings beyond the Lion and Lamb seem to have been held continuously by 'Mrs. Smith' until 1835.

(2) Will of Samuel Smith of the City of York Gardener (Borthwick Institute: York Prerogative Wills, May 1757).

Whereas I have surrendered all my estate at Holgate within the Manor of Acomb to the use of my last will I devise the same to my niece Isabel Hodgson her heirs etc. according to the custom of the Manor
all the residue to my two sisters Mary Mattison and Ann Pulleyn and my said niece Isabel Hodgson equally
to my nephew William Smith 20s. to my nephew John Smith 20s.
my two sisters and my niece to be my Executrices
Signed and sealed by Samll Smith 30 January 1756
Witnesses: J. Ricard Mary Kilvington Thos. Vevers
Proved 28 May 1757
Bond of Mary Mattison of the City of York widow John Pulleyn of the same Mariner Isabel Hodgson of the same spinster and William Hesletine of the same Gardiner in £200 for due execution 28 May 1757 the said Mary Mattison Ann wife of the above John Pulleyn and Isabel Hodgson being Joint Executrixes
the mark of Mary X Mattison signatures of the others

Samuel Smith (c. 1695-1757), son of William Smith 'chymist' of York, took up the freedom of the city as a gardener in 1716. He was Chamberlain of York in 1741 and in that year was a voter, as of Micklegate Bar (Poll Book). As a nurseryman and florist he was an early advertiser, twice inserting in the *York Courant* (7 and 14 April 1730) a notice that at his 'Flower Garden without Michael-gate Bar, York, is to be seen a choice Collection of Ariculas, Animonies, Renunculos, Tulops and other Flowers ... where any Persons may be furnish'd with the best and newest Flowers, at reasonable Rates.' He supplied trees in 1732 for finishing the New Walk by the River Ouse and was paid £12.2s.6d. by the Corporation (York City Archives, C.34, f. 9v). In 1755 he bought the estate in Holgate mentioned in his will, consisting of a messuage and 2½ acres of land in the occupation of William Calvert (H. Richardson, ed., *Court Rolls of the Manor of Acomb,* Yorkshire Archaeological Society, Record Series, cxxxi, 1969, 243, 245). His gardens off Blossom Street behind the sites of nos. 21-29 passed after his death into the successive occupations of the gardeners George Hargraves and John Roebuck (Appendix B.2 above).

(3) As an example of a will containing unusually precise details of the history of houses, an extract is given below from that of Thomas Wolstenholme (1759-1812), a York carver (Borthwick Institute, York Prerogative Wills, Register 1813, f. 514).

I Thomas Wolstenholme of Bootham near the City of York   Carver ... from the beneficence of my Creator have been blessed with Health and Genius which aided by Industry and Economy enabled me in the year 1790 to purchase of Mr. John Hudson a freehold estate situated at the corner of Bootham and Gillygate in the parish of St. Giles consisting of two dwelling houses Coach-House Stables ... upon part of which premises in the year 1797 I built two houses fronting into Gillygate and also in the year 1799 erected a small house facing into Bootham at the same time raised one of the aforementioned adjoining old houses a story higher ...

to my natural daughter Arabella Poole who now lives with me the northeast house of the aforesaid in Gillygate adjoining to Mr. Hugh Footell's premises ... to my Father Ely Wolstenholme the next adjoining south-west house ... with all its conveniences as now finishing for my own residence

to my brother Dean Wolstenholme the corner house of Bootham and Gillygate up to the walls of the last mentioned buildings with all conveniences ... as at present enjoyed by him and my father as Tenants to me

to my sole surviving sister Elizabeth the wife of Thomas Walker the house adjoining to the last mentioned in Bootham as enjoyed by her and her husband as tenants to me

to Francis Wolstenholme my youngest brother the house and offices left to my father in Gillygate at my father's death ...

to Arabella Poole my personal property furniture linen clothing books drawings prints china plate cash bills bonds etc. ...

to Francis Wolstenholme the succession of my Business in Composition Ornaments Carving and Gilding with all the Stock in hand moulds drawing tools books and every other article used in conducting the same belonging to me in the shops or places at the manor (i.e. The King's Manor, York) or elsewhere ....

to Thomas Walker husband of my sister Elizabeth for his attention to my interest in conducting my joiner work all the timber   deals or other materials as stock on hand with the lathe   benches   tools and every other thing both in the Workshops and elsewhere ... which appertained to that Branch of Business.

my Brothers Dean and Francis Wolstenholme to be Executors

signed by Thomas Wolstenholme   26 July 1800

Witnesses: Michael Taylor ` Robert Tomlinson   Jno. Hodgson

Past 23 February 1813.

Ely Wolstenholme the father (1724-1810), a weaver and fringe manufacturer, died two years before Thomas. The houses built by Thomas Wolstenholme in 1797 were nos. 3 and 5, Gillygate; the small house in Bootham built in 1799 is numbered 15 and 17.

APPENDIX D

LEASES

Leases of house property, especially when preserved in a continuous series, are among the most valuable sources. They usually give a fairly detailed description of the property let and often name earlier occupiers. In the case of leasehold properties belonging to ancient collegiate foundations the traditional rents, including those paid partly in kind, frequently survived down to modern times. Examples of this will be found below (1) in a series of extracts from the lease registers of the Vicars Choral of York Minster (Minster Library, Sub-Chanter's Books, vols. 1-6, Audit Book). A different type is the building lease, in which the construction of a house or other building is part of the consideration for which the lease is granted. An early and unusually detailed building lease appears below (2).

(1) The York Vicars Choral owned many small properties scattered through the city, and among them two in the parish of Holy Trinity in the upper part of Micklegate (modern nos. 112, 116). A full abstract of the most recent lease of no. 112 (Book 6, p. 133) is followed by brief particulars in reverse chronological order.

1854 May 10 Renewed to Elizabeth Mark widow of Thomas Mark of Workington Cumberland the lease of a messuage now used as a Public House called the Red Lion and three cottages and a Stable behind in Micklegate and extending to Toft Green which were in the occupation of Catherine Cowgill then of Thomas Kilvington, Richard Scaife, Richard Standys and John Cundell and now of — Archbell, — Richardson and — Cundell
for 40 years from 26 February last
Rent 7s. and 2 fat hens.   Fine £56.0.0
Lease last renewed to Thomas Mark and Elizabeth his wife on 7 January 1841   (Book 6, 1847-65, p. 133)

1841 Jan 29 Renewed to Thomas Mark of Workington and his wife Elizabeth (as above) now in the occupation of Thomas Kilvington and others 40 years from 26 Feb 1840   same Rent and Fine
Last renewed to said Thomas Mark and wife 11 May 1826 (Book 5, 288)

1826 May 11 Renewed to Thomas Mark grocer and his wife Elizabeth (as above) now in the occupation of Thomas Kilvington, William Hasselwood, Richard Standidge and John Cundill   for 40 years from 26 Feb 1826   same Rent   Fine £49.7s.0d.
Last renewed to Mrs. Ann Bulmer 26 Feb 1812   (Book 5, p. 105)

1812 Feb 26 Renewed to Ann Bulmer of Holgate widow the daughter of John Allanson late of Holgate esq. formerly of York merchant the lease of a messuage in Micklegate and backwards to Toft Green late in the occupation of Catherine Cowgill   for 40 years
Rent 7s. and 2 fat hens   Fine £330.0.0*
Last renewed to John Allanson 18 Oct 1774   (Book 4, p. 296)
*The reason for this very large fine is not known; it may imply rebuilding.

46

1774 Oct 18   Renewed to John Allanson junior a lease for 40 years of a messuage in Micklegate formerly in the occupation of Richard Birkley, Francis Wickan, Mary Rudd and Mary Ward, late in the occupation of John Mawson and now of Elizabeth (?) Crabtree widow   same Rent   Fine £17
Last renewed to John Allanson alderman 2 Jan 1759   (Book 3, p.232)

1759 Jan 2   John Allanson esq., the Lord Mayor, renewed Lease for 40 years of Messuage in Micklegate (It is a long, narrow piece of ground, chiefly cover'd with Buildings; abutting at one end on Micklegate, and at the other on Toft Green). The whole is rented by Joseph Morson, Bricklayer, who lets off divers parts. That part which is occupied by Ezekiel Storky was rebuilt since our last Renewal.
Same Rent   Fine £12
Renewal on 14 Aug 1744 to Mrs. Ann Benson, widow   (Book 3, p.75)

1744 Aug 14   Mrs. Ann Benson, widow, renewd ye lease of a tenement in Micklegate late in the occupation of Mr. William Benson - Above 13 years expired in old lease.
Same rent   Fine £10   (Book 2, p. 427)

1731 July 9   Renewal tŏ Mr. William Benson son of Mr. Jonathan Benson (as above) for 40 years - formerly in Mr. Richard Benson's name 21 July 1716   Fine £10   (Book 2, p. 269)

1716 July 21   Mr. Richard Benson   Lease of tenement in Mickle Gate for 40 years - formerly taken by Ald. Wood - 14 years expir'd very near.   Fine £7.10.0   (Book 2, p.130)

1702 Aug 7   John Wood, Alderman, renewed lease of a tenement in Micklegate for 40 years - 14 years expired   Fine £7.10.0   (Book 2, p. 32)

1688 Oct 12   Mr. John Wood renewing lease of a house in Micklegt. taken in his own name and his daughter Dorothy's - 5¼ years expired   Fine £2.10.0   (Book 1, p. 267)

1683 June 11   Mr. John Wood, Ald., (Fine) £7.10.0 for house in Micklegt. taken before in the name of Mrs. Margaret Bean, now in his own name and his daughter Margarett's - almost 12 years expired   (Book 1, p. 231)

1671 Aug 31   Mrs. Margrett Beane's Lease renewed - 6 years expired   Fine £1.10.0   (Book 1, p. 99)

As a commentary upon the difficulty of establishing the real occupiers of houses it is worth giving the sequence of ratepayers assessed to this house, no. 112 Micklegate, in the Rate Assessments for the parish of Holy Trinity. In 1774 the valuation was £10 and Mrs. Mawson was named; from 1775 her place was taken by Mr. Joseph Donnison, but from 1779-80 at the reduced assessment of £3. From 1795 two figures appear, of £3 and £1, and until 1812-

13 the ratepayer was Mr. Cogill or Cowgill for both, but on the £1 rating he paid 'for Mr. Allison' or Allanson. In 1810-11, however, the name against the £3 assessment was 'Mr. Wood'. This appears as Edward Woods from 1813, while John Cundle, Cundale, Cundall or Cundill was rated on £1 until 1838, for a house, though Mr. Allanson appears at this figure in 1820-22. From 1819 to 1823 the ratepayer on £3 was Mrs. Johnson, except for 1820-21, when the name is Mr. Hansom. From 1823 to 1838 continuously this section of the premises, clearly identifiable as the Red Lion public house, was rated in the name of Thomas Kilvington, known from other sources to have succeeded Ann Johnson as the licensee. Kilvington was succeeded by Robert Bean and Bean, in 1850, by James Sowden. It will have been noted that Mrs. Ann Johnson, evidenced in Baines's Directory of 1823 as victualler of the Red Lion, and the actual ratepayer named in the parish assessments, is not mentioned at all in any of the leases. In 1835-36 part of the property was described as house and stables at a valuation of £4.10.0 and the ratepayer was E. Woods, but his name does not appear again. At a revaluation of the parish in 1838 the Red Lion, as public house and stables, was put at £14.9.0, a house of John Cundill at £5.2.0, and there were two smaller tenements each rated on £3.8.0 in the occupation of John Thackray and of Richard Standish. In 1840 *Robert* Scaife took the place of Thackray, to be succeeded in rapid succession by Thomas Freeman, Charles Cowper, Elizabeth Hodgson and (in 1850) William Wilson. The second of the two small tenements was 'late Richard Standish' by 1845, then Robert Weymouth, and from 1849 James Richardson. At this later period there is a substantial correspondence with the occupiers named in the leases, but it is impossible to distinguish clearly which parts of the property formed their dwellings. By 1759 or even earlier the lessees had ceased altogether to be occupiers of any part of the premises.

(2) The manor of Eling, Hants., formed part of the original endowment of Winchester College in 1385. A manorial corn-mill had anciently stood on a causeway crossing a tidal inlet at the head of Southampton Water, and the mill-wheels were driven by the ebb and flow of the tide to and from a reservoir formed by the causeway. This causeway and mill had long been in ruin and it was not until about 1415 that the Warden and Fellows, as Lords of the Manor, began to seek a means of arranging for rebuilding (T. F. Kirby, *Annals of Winchester College,* 1892, 186-7). The building lease granted survives as an original and as a counterpart, the date being given as Christmas Day 1418 in the counterpart but as 1417 over an erasure in the lease (Winchester College Muniments nos. 26454-55). Below is an English abstract from the Latin original.

This indenture made between Robert Thurbern Warden of the College called 'Seint Marie College of Wynchestre' near the City of Winchester on the one part and Thomas Midlyngton burgess of the town of Southampton on the other part witnesses that the foresaid Warden by assent and consent of the fellows and scholars of the same College has let granted and demised to the foresaid Thomas all the site or ground with the pond and fishing adjoining on which of old the mill of Eling was set   to have and to hold the whole ... to the foresaid Thomas his heirs and assigns from the day of the making of these presents to the end of the term of fifty years then next following ... And the foresaid Thomas his heirs or executors upon the said site or ground shall cause to be made anew at their own costs and expenses within two years now next following a good and competent watermill with all and singular necessaries that belong and are needful to such a mill together with a good and sufficient house competently covered with 'sclattes shingels or reede' the foundations and walls of which mill on all sides shall be of hewn stones sufficiently laid and set with lime and sand both inside and out which walls shall be of competent thickness and so high that the sea at full flood shall not overflow the foresaid walls   Rendering thence yearly after the first year of the foresaid term of fifty years to the foresaid Warden and his successors at the feast of the Lord's Nativity 13 shillings and 4 pence during the foresaid term   And the foresaid Warden or his successors shall pay to the same Thomas his heirs or executors in aid of the making of the foresaid works 20 marks (£13.6s.8d.) within the four first years after the building and final construction of the mill and of the foresaid works namely in each year at the feast of the Lord's Nativity 5 marks sterling without further delay and to this the foresaid Warden binds himself and his successors by these presents the which mill with all its necessaries when it shall have been built the foresaid Thomas his heirs and executors or assigns shall well and competently sustain maintain and repair from year to year and from time to time at their own costs and expenses during the foresaid term of fifty years and at the end of the same term shall render it up well and competently repaired with all its necessaries in good and competent state so that it may in all likelihood last for seven years then immediately following after the said term of fifty years 'le Goynggere' (going gear) through sudden fire hostile invasion and reasonable use however excepted   And if it shall happen that the foresaid rent ... should be in arrear wholly or in part for twenty-six weeks after the foresaid feast of the Nativity ... and shall be publicly demanded or the repair and due maintenance of the said mill with all its necessaries for twenty-six weeks after being required ... then it shall be lawful for the said Warden ... to re-enter ... and take back into his hands and possess it in peace this lease notwithstanding   And the foresaid Warden and his successors warrant to the foresaid Thomas ... the foresaid site or ground with the pond and fishing adjoining ... against all people during the foresaid term   Moreover the foresaid Thomas considering that a certain causeway and bridges in the same causeway for footmen and horsemen built of old lying between Eling and Totton has long been broken down and left in disrepair by the flow of the sea and by great storms to the serious damage of the people there passing across whose building and repair as it is said were wont to be made by the alms of the people of that country from a time beyond memory has to the honour of God by reason of charity of his own motion on behalf of the salvation of his soul and of the soul of Margaret late his wife and of the souls of their parents friends and benefactors granted and promised to make anew and repair the foresaid Causeway sufficiently for footmen and horsemen within two years next following after the date of these presents without placing timber in the same unless in places where timber must needs be placed so that the said Causeway according to human discretion shall be likely to last for a hundred years now to come   Provided only that the workmen and craftsmen hired by the foresaid Thomas to make the foresaid works of the mill and of the foresaid Causeway be not arrested by the officers of the lord King or hindered or removed from that work and he shall not be able to find other workmen and craftsmen to make and complete those works within the foresaid two years from this cause then the same Thomas shall make and in all things complete the foresaid works in as short a time as he can And the foresaid Warden has granted for himself and his successors to the foresaid Thomas ... in aid of the repair and making of the foresaid Mill and Causeway licence to dig and take clay and sand sufficient within the soil of the manor of Eling where it may seem most convenient to the foresaid Thomas

In witness of which to the part of this indenture remaining with the foresaid Warden the foresaid Thomas has set his seal and because the seal of the foresaid Thomas is to many unknown the seal of the Mayoralty of the town of Southampton at the special request of the same Thomas is set to the same part and to 'the part of this indenture remaining with the foresaid Thomas the foresaid Warden by the assent and consent of the foresaid fellows and scholars has set their common seal to these presents Given in the foresaid College on the feast of the Lord's Nativity in the year of the reign of King Henry the fifth after the conquest of England the sixth and A. D. 1418.

APPENDIX E

SURVEYS

Surveys in written form were made long before trigonometrical surveying with plane-table or theodolite made accurate maps and plans a possibility. Without plans to scale it was essential that a written survey should be detailed and precise, and there was therefore a long tradition of compilation which only slowly gave way after plans had made much of the detail unnecessary. Although directed mainly towards description of land, surveys often give valuable details of houses and of other buildings. The information given is usually precisely dated, but sometimes facts relating to earlier owners or occupiers, or to the title deeds, may be given.

(1)   Two extracts are given below from the Parliamentary Survey of Church Lands made in 1649-50 upon the 'Act of the Commons of England ... for the abolishinge of Deanes, Deanes and Chapters, Cannons, Prebends and other Offices and Titles of and belonginge to any Cathedrall or Collegiate Church or Chappell within England and Wales'. The extracts concern houses belonging to the Prebends or to the Dean and Chapter of York Minster.

(a)   A Survey of the Mannor and Prebend of Bechill and Knaresbrough in the countye of Yorke late belonginge to the prebendary of Knaresbrough ... 16th Aprill 1650 ...
The Mannor howse consisteth of a Kitchine a parlor, a little Butterie, a Milkehowse one other parlor devided into twoe Chambers &c.
(Memorandum that Daniel Lyndley of Terrington, Yorks., clerk, prebendary

of Knaresbrough in the Cathedral Church of York, had on 20 January 1622/3 demised to Sir Henry Slingsby of Scriven the prebend with all tithes and profits at a Rent of £45 a year, for the three lives of Henry Slingsby son and heir of the said Sir Henry, Thomas Slingsby his second son, and Robert Stapleton son of Brian Stapleton of Myton, Yorks., Esq. and the life of the longest liver of them; and that Henry Slingsby the son was aged 48, Thomas Slingsby 45 and that Robert Stapleton is living in Ireland.)

The Viccaridge of Knaresbrough

The Viccaridge howse consisteth of an Entrie an Hall, a Parlor, a Butterie devided into twoe over which three Chambers, a Clossett and a Studdie, alsoe a Kitchine and other twoe little Lowe Roomes, over which other twoe Chambers with a Barne in good repaire, wth a Garden and Orchard with a passage to the same and to the howse, scituate betwixt A Tenement of William Comers gent. on the West and a Tenement of Thomas Headon on the East ... (with tithes of the townships of Knaresbrough parish worth in common years 50s.) The Right of presentacion hath beene formerly in the prebendary, but hee not excepting the same in his graunt to the Lessee, the Lessee by a tryall att Lawe recovered the presentacion, and accordingly presented on Mr. Attie, but the now present Incumbent is Mr. Mathew Booth.

(b)   A Survey of the Rectorie or Parsonage of Copmanthorpe ... in the Countye and Cittye of Yorke late parcell of the possessions belonginge to the Deane and Chapter of St. Peeters in Yorke ... (13th) Aprill 1650 ...
One Tenement or Howse called the parsonage howse consistinge of a Little porch, five small Lowe Roomes, a Little passage or entrye one meane Chamber with a fold yard, in wch one Large Tithe Barne now built with a little garthe on the Backside of the said howse abutting on the Fold yard and one the North end of the said Barne lyeinge beetwixt the Lands of Henry Fenton on the East and the Lands of Thomas Wealbye on the west cont(aining) by estim(acion) 1 Rood   (valued at) 26s. 8d.

One other Tenement commonly called the Viccaridge howse consistinge an Entrie   Foure Lowe Roomes   three Chambers   a Barne and Beast howse with a Fold yard and one outhowse on the backside wth a Chamber over it all in good repaire   a Little Orchard and a verry small backside lyeinge betwixt the Lands of Henry Fenton on the East, and the Lands of Thomas Wealby on the west   Conteyning altogether by estimacion 1 Rood   (valued at) 20s.
(Memorandum that George Meriton D.D., Dean and the Chapter, had by indenture of 4 March 1618/19 demised the Rectory or Parsonage of Copmanthorpe to Robert Sprignaell of Highgate in the parish of Hornsey in the County of Middlesex Esqr. for the lives of Richard Sprignaell his son and heir and of Frances Sprignaell and Suzanna Sprignaell daughters of the said Robert Sprignaell and the life of the longest liver of them at a Rent of £16 a year, but that the property is worth upon improvement £68.18s.3d. over and above the said Rent per annum.)
(Lambeth Palace Library, Survey of Church Lands, vol. 17 (Cod. Lambeth 918), ff. 220-5, 463-6)

(2)   The extract below describes the old manor house of Great Bookham, Surrey, long since demolished, as it was in 1615, when a detailed survey book and a scale plan were made by Thomas Clay, one of the earliest scientific land surveyors (see J. H. Harvey in *Proceedings of the Leatherhead and District Local History Society,* ii no. 10, 1966, 281-3).

Demaines

Robert Marshe holdeth by Indenture of lease the Mannour house or Capitall Messuage called Bookeham Courte well and sufficiently builte and covered with Tyle together with the other buildings and outhouses belonging to the same viz. 2 greate Barnes wherof one covered with tyle and sufficiently boarded rounde aboute contayneing (blank) bayes and the other covered with thatche and walled about with loame contayneing (blank) Bayes   one Stable covered with thatche contayneing (blank) Bayes   one Stalle or Oxehouse contayneing (blank) Bayes   a gatehouse and a granarie on ye south side of the Courte covered with tyle the gatehouse being now much in decay and with age and for want of reparacion ready to fall: which said Mannour house and buildings to the same belonging together with the greate yard or gate there and the gardens and Orchard therunto appertayneing are scituate in Greate Bookeham aforesaid neere unto the Church there ... and contayne in all 2 roodes 36 perches.

(Great Bookham Manorial Records of the National Trust, now deposited in the Surrey Record Office, Survey Book, f. 14)

APPENDIX F

COURT ROLLS

The evidence of manorial Court Rolls, so far as copyhold premises are concerned, is important for its continuity. The succession of tenants is recorded without any break, though it has to be borne in mind that, as with leaseholds, the actual occupiers may have been sub-tenants. Licences to sub-let had generally to be obtained, and commonly name the parties. Permission to build on the waste land of the manor was recorded, and entries of this kind give the date when a house was first built on a site hitherto vacant. At times evidences of title to freeholds attached to the manor were enrolled: in such instances the court rolls served as a register of deeds (see above, Appendix B). Among the most useful entries are the pains laid upon tenants, ordering them to carry out repairs to houses and barns. Instances of all these types of record are found in the first ten years to survive of the court rolls of Great Bookham, Surrey (The National Trust, Great Bookham Common documents, now deposited in Surrey Record Office, Roll A, 1554-1616).

(1) Permission to build a house on the waste, Court held 15 April 1556.
To this Court came John Arnold and sought licence from the lord to build a house on the common of Great Bookham in a certain place there next 'le Slade Bushes', and thereupon his Steward by assent of the tenants there assigned to the same John half an acre of land in the common of Bookham aforesaid in a certain place there next to the common of Little Bookham next 'le Slade Bushes'   To have to him and his heirs at the will of the lord according to the custom of the manor by copy of Court Roll by rent of 8d. a year and suit of Court, and for having title of his right there he gives to the lord for Fine two capons and for Fine Certain after (any) alienation two fat capons

(2)   Registration of title to a freehold, Court held 7 October 1556.
Alienation of a free tenement   To this Court came Henry Marter and proferred here in Court a certain charter of his granted to him by Thomas Dudley and sought that it should be enrolled   the purport of which charter follows viz. To all the faithful in Christ to whom this present charter shall come, I Thomas Dudley of Effingham in the County of Surrey wheelwright, perpetual greeting in the Lord   Know that I the foresaid Thomas Dudley for ten pounds of lawful money of England to me by Henry Marter the son of Thomas Marter of Effingham in the County of Surrey in hand paid of which etc. (i.e. receipt is acknowledged) have given granted and by this my present charter have confirmed to the foresaid Henry Marter all that my messuage with a garden and four acres of land set lying and being in Eastwick in the parish of Great Bookham in the said County of Surrey   To have and to hold the foresaid messuage with its appurtenances to the foresaid (blank) to the use and behoof of the same Henry his heirs and assigns for ever of the capital etc. (i.e. lords of this fee)   And I etc. against all people etc. (i.e. give warranty)   Given the (blank) day of October in the years of King Philip and Queen Mary by the grace of God etc. the second and third (October 1555).

(3)   Licence to let and order to repair, Court of 10 October 1558.
Licence   John Gardiner junior seeks licence to let at farm to Richard Blundell all his customary lands and tenements held of this manor from Michaelmas next (29 September 1559) for six years - Fine 3s. 4d.
A Day is given to the same John to repair his tenement now very ruinous and he begs that timber may be assigned to him by the Lord's bailiff - three trees (probably oak trees)

(4)   Repeated orders to repair:

(a)   Court held 29 October 1554
Also they (the manorial jury) present that John Dendy has forfeited 40d. part of his pain laid on him at the last Court because he has not repaired his tenement in great decay ... and a further day is given to the same John to repair the said tenement before the feast of All Saints next (1 November !) on pain of 6s. 8d.

(b)   Court held 30 September 1557

Pain   The Homage present that the house of John Dendy is greatly ruinous and in decay both in timber and in roofing with straw   Therefore a day is given to the same John for the sufficient repair and amendment of the said house in all things before the feast of the Annunciation of the Blessed Virgin Mary next (25 March 1558) on pain of   20s.

(c)   Court held 30 March 1558

Forfeiture; pain   Also they present that John Dendy has forfeited part of the pain laid on him in the last Court because he has not repaired his tenement according to the pain laid on him in the last Court   and therefore a new day is given to the same John for the sufficient repair of the said tenement in all things before the feast of St. Michael the Archangel (29 September 1558) next on pain of   26s. 8d.

(d)   Court held 10 October 1558

A day is given to John Dendy for the sufficient mending and repair of his tenement now very ruinous before Easter next (26 March 1559) on pain of   40s.

(5)   Licence to take down and remove part of a (timber framed) house, and to re-erect elsewhere, Court held 6 October 1614

Licence   Thomas Wood of Bagden was granted licence to take down the west end of a certain tenement of his called Tanners and to rebuild the same at his tenement called Bagden before the feast of St. John Baptist next (24 June 1615) - Fine 6s.

(6)   Prosecutions for taking in lodgers (Court Book, 1621-1642)

(a)   View of Frankpledge held 2 October 1628 (f. 36v)

Mary Hilder of Bookham aforesaid widow did on 1 September 1628 take receive and maintain ... Richard Lock and his family to dwell with her in one house as subtenants called 'Inmates'.

(b)   View of Frankpledge held 2 October 1629 (f. 40v)

Edward Cock on the 1 September 1629 received a stranger ... Richard Lock etc.

(c)   View of Frankpledge held 7 October 1630 (f. 44-44v)

Edmond Hudson has received Edward Bonyan

Thomas Twyne has received John Port as a subtenant

William Waker has received William Babb as an inmate

Robert Marsh has received (blank)

George Sheires of Slyfield esquire having a cottage at Northend let it to Andrew Barnes a stranger without giving security to the Overseers of the Poor - Fine £10

Richard Sheppard has received Laurence Fenn

Thomas Peeter has received Edward Wilkyn
Richard Sheppard vitler has lodged Jane Prine of ill and incontinent life

(d)   View of Frankpledge held 7 October 1634 (f. 60)
Subtenants   Christopher Hiller has received John Wilking and John Peeter
Inmates   William Babb has received John Stevens and Edward Shute

APPENDIX G
INVENTORIES

The importance of detailed inventories as historical evidence for artistic
purposes has always been recognized, and more recently the study of large
numbers of probate inventories has provided a basis for statistical inquiries
into social history. Here we are concerned only with the specific evidence
which may be obtained regarding individual houses and the families who lived
in them. One inventory of the late eighteenth century, in association with the
will of a York gardener, has already been given (Appendix C). Unfortunately
surviving inventories are very irregularly distributed over the country, and in
many areas few or no probate inventories survive. When found, inventories
may vary from the short and uninformative to the forbiddingly detailed,
running to many pages or membranes of parchment. Below are given two
examples of Elizabethan inventories of Surrey villagers, and an extract from a
printed sale catalogue which forms an inventory of 1767.

(1)   A very short inventory annexed to the will of John Hubbard (Hibbard,
Hybarde) of Great Bookham, Surrey, yeoman, made 26 April 1588 and
proved 17 May 1591. The inventory, made by Ralph Crowcher and John
Dudley on 14 May 1591, describes the testator as 'husbondman': both
assessors sign by mark, and their valuation was written down by William
Cooke scrivener.

Brass		
1 old 'Caldren' ('cauderne' in the will)	6s.	8d.
2 brass Pots	8s.	
a little broken pan		4d.
Pewter		
3 old platters	1s.	
3 new platters	2s.	8d.
2 dishes & 2 sasers	1s.	8d.
Apparell		
1 old chest with apparell	13s.	4d.
Sheep		
2 Eawe sheepe	6s.	8d.
2 Teggs (second-year sheep)	6s.	8d.

(2)   The much more detailed inventory of Henry Wilkins, also of Great Bookham and likewise a husbandman, can be given a background from court rolls and other documents and relates to a surviving timber-framed house, 'Woodcote', Lower Road, Bookham, at the corner of Eastwick Road (Hampshire Record Office, Winchester Consistory Court, Original Wills and Inventories, and registered will of Wilkins, Reg. 1, f. 10). In 1524 Richard Wylkyn and Agnes his wife, of Great Bookham, paid 1s. to the lay subsidy; their son was Bartholomew Wilkyns, one of the homage at the first surviving Court of the Manor of Eastwick in Bookham, held 5 March 1539/40 (Surrey Record Office, Manor of Eastwick 1540-1612). At a Court held 6 May 1544 Bartholomew Wilkyn surrendered his tenement garden and 14 acres in Eastwick and Great Bookham to his wife Anne until Henry Wilkyn came to the age of 16 years. On 5 January 1558/9 Henry Wilkyn son of Bartholomew was admitted to the property on payment of a fine of 20s. On 18 December 1575 'Harrie Wilkins' of Eastwick in Great Bookham made his will, leaving his tenement in Eastwick to his son John Wilkins when 21, but 'my wife Margaret' to have the occupying of it. There were three other children. John was to have 'a great caudron the wch my mother gave me' and 'the cobbard in the hall and the table standing on a frame in the hall.' The will was proved on 10 May 1576.

Inventory taken 25 January 1576 of all goods of Henrie Wilkyns of Estwycke in the parish of great Buckeham ... husbandman praysed (appraised) by Raphe Stevens, John Gardener and John Bythewood and Thomas Stambridge.

The haule   Imprimis A table standing one a forme being a stander of the howse also one old forme to the tabell belonginge   2s.
Item a Joyned cobberd   4s.
Item a potte hanger in the chymny   4d.
Item 2 old stolles (stools)   1d.
Item the paynted clothes (wall hangings)   4d.

The Kytchen   First a cawdran wth a bayll (handle) like a kettell verie old   2s. 6d.
Item a posnett wth 3 litle skilletts   2s. 6d.
Item 8 old platters   2s. 8d.
Item 3 dishes   6d.
Item 3 sawcers   6d.
Item an old grydyron   2d.
Item a spitte   3d.
Item 2 candelsticks   4d.
Item old Tubbes   20d.

The chamber   First 2 old matrisses   16d.
Item 2 paynted testers wth the clothes about the chamber   2s. 6d.
Item 2 blaincketts 2 coverletts   2s. 6d.
Item 3 payre of sheatts 2 old table clothes   4s.
Item 2 old chests   2s. 8d.

Wearing geare   First a cote a Jurkyne a payre of hoosse a cavis
(canvas) shurt   6s. 4d.

Item in his purse   12d.

The Barne   First by estimacion 20 buschells of Wheat and Rye   40s.
Item in barlie by estimacion   33s. 4d.
Item in hay and Tarres (tares)   10s.
Item an old phane (winnowing fan) and an old busshell without eares 8d.
Item in fyve acres of winter corne being Wheat and Rye being now
soene one the ground   33s. 4d.

The Cattle   First 3 mayres   33s. 4d.
Item one cowe and a bullocke and a weaner of this yere   26s. 8d.
Item 2 hoogg shutes   4s.
Item an old cart and thereunto belonging   10s.
Item bacon in the Rooffe   2s.

Total 11.^{li} 11.^{s} 8.^{d}

(3) The house and furniture of James Clarke, a bankrupt nurseryman of Dorking, Surrey, were sold at auction on 24 April 1767. The printed catalogue of the sale (Public Record Office, C110/174) lists the whole of the furniture room by room. The rooms named were Garret on the right hand, Back Kitchen, Passage, Still-House, Chamber over the Parlour, Back Room over the Stable, Back Room leading to the Garden, Back Garret, Parlour, Shop, Little Room by the Shop, Chamber over the Shop, Wash-House, Staircase, Chamber over the Back Kitchen, Chamber over the Kitchen, Kitchen. The details of lots in three rooms are reprinted below.

Chamber over the Parlour

41   A bedstead with blue harateen furniture.
42   A goose featherbed bolster and three pillows.
43   A check quilt and three blankets.
44   A wainscot chest of drawers.
45   A walnut tree table and swing glass.
46   Five ash chairs with matted seats and a chest.
47   Ten prints framed.
48   A side saddle and cloth.

Parlour

94   A stove with brass furniture.
95   A fire shovel, a pair of tongs, a poker, and a pair of bellows.
96   Six walnut tree chairs.
97   A ditto scrutore with glass doors.
98   A mahogany oval dining table.
99   A ditto pillar and claw with green cloth.
100 A japan'd corner cupboard and a broken glass.
101 Some pieces of oil cloth and 11 prints glazed.
102 A hearth with a brass front.

Chamber over the Shop

121   A large stove, fender, shovel, poker, and a pair of bellows.
122   A large square table.
123   A pier glass in a painted frame.
124   A spinnet in a japan case, by Bradshaw, Lond.
125   A Japan case with a glass door.
126   A walnut tree cloaths press ornamented with black ebony.
127   An oak desk, a frame, two chairs, a back gammon box.
128   Five chairs, two pair of green window curtains and rods.
129   An oak cupboard, a pistol, two sconces, and a piece of painting.
130   Some curious sea shells.

BOOKS

131   One bible and four other books.
132   Ditto.
133   English traveller, 3 Volumes.
134   —Tradesman and 4 others.
135   The London spy and 3 of Shakespear's plays.
136   Bailey's Dictionary and 6 others.
137   Nelson's Justice and 6 others.
138   — Fast and 6 others.
139   Some bound books.
140   Ditto.

INDEX

BRITISH RECORDS ASSOCIATION

The British Records Association was founded in November 1932 as a national organization to co-ordinate and encourage the work of the many individuals, authorities, institutions and societies interested in the conservation and use of records.

Its aims are:

(i) *Co-operation.* The Association serves as a link between all who are concerned in the ownership, custody, preservation, study and publication of records. Its journal *ARCHIVES* is issued twice yearly.

(ii) *Preservation of Records.* It seeks to develop informed opinion on the necessity for preserving records of historical importance and the means by which this can be achieved. It will advise on the disposal of papers, deeds and documents of all kinds through its Records Preservation Section. It makes available technical information in collaboration with the Society of Archivists.

(iii) *Utilization of Records.* It furthers the use of records as historical material, particularly through the medium of publication.

MEMBERSHIP

Membership is open to any individual or institution interested in records and in the aims of the Association. All who care for the history of Britain as reflected in its wealth of records are invited to join. Applications for enrolment and all enquiries concerning the Association should be addressed to the Honorary Secretary, British Records Association, Master's Court, The Charterhouse, Charterhouse Square, London, EC1M 6AU.